한라아리랑

Halla Arirang

제주 밭담에서

난 보았습니다

내 눈썹보다 약간 높은 하늘과
아기 솜털 같은 하얀 구름
세미소 오름길 따라서
철부지 바람이랑
종달새가 노래를 하고
철쭉꽃이 피는 한라산
파도 일렁이는 바다 사이
해 오르는 섬으로
푸른빛 청보리가 춤실데는
그 길로 가면

진 검은 밭담 틈 사이
난 보았습니다

붙들린 이 내 마음은

떠나온
머언 고향

지난 청춘―,
언제나 그 기억에서

조용히 앉아
내 무딘 가슴 움켜잡지요

인생길

끝없는 길
나는 걷노라

이 길을 가고 있는데
설령 누군가 막는다 해도
곧바로 난 가리라

그 길에 마주치는
많은 것들
폭설과 소나기를 맞아도
뜨거운 태양 아래에서도
누더기 된 옷을 걸치고서
나는 걸으리라

그대 사랑 속에서 힘이 솟는다
흰머리가 되어 다 빠지고
무릎 골이 닳아 통증이 저려와도
그대 사랑 속에서 곧바로 그 길을 완주하리라

나 하나가

나 하나가
나룻배로 단단해져서
당신이 이 깊은 강 건널 수 있게 해주시오

나 하나가
다리가 되어 무사히
당신이 건너올 수 있게 해주시오

나 하나가 다른 몸을 입는다면
그것으로
당신이 내게로 오는 길이 되는 까닭이오

청춘의 숲에서

어느 해, 산책을 나선 길
걷다 보니
안개 자욱한 숲속이었네

숲속을 지날 때,
짙은 향기에 발길을 멈추고
미지의 자연은 가지각색으로
나에게 가까이 다가왔네

모든 것들은 신비로움으로 가득한데
더는 숲으로 깊숙이
나는 갈 수가 없었다네

그곳에서 머물 수 없는 까닭은
아직 나의 청춘이 많이 남아 있기
때문이었네

한
라
아
리
랑

Halla Arirang

c
h
e
d
a
n
g

차례

1부 빈집

2 / 제주 밭담에서
3 / 붙들린 이 내 마음은
4 / 인생길
5 / 나 하나가
6 / 청춘의 숲에서
12 / 인연
14 / 동백화
16 / 제주 바람꽃
18 / 기억의 등을
밝히는 말
24 / 그 비
26 / 가얏고
28 / 둘이서 가까이
하고픈 까닭은
30 / 첫연가
32 / 고독
34 / 청보리 소리
36 / 향수병
38 / 고향의 서
40 / 국화꽃 향기 앞에서
44 / 광복의 날
46 / 빈집

2부 천걸음

52 / 사모 1
54 / 바다를 끓이다
56 / 유산
58 / 거대한 산
60 / 아버지의 기억
62 / 한라산 편지
66 / 그냥
68 / 공양
70 / 천걸음
73 / 바다가 웃는다
75 / 독백
78 / 아름다운 날에
82 / 비의 회억
84 / 사모 2
86 / 사랑을 위하여
잠못 이루는 벗에게
90 / 가을의 기도
92 / 무궁화
93 / 장 속의 새

3부 한라아리랑   4부 인생만곡

96 / 한라 아리랑
98 / 죽도록
100 / 슬픈자화상
104 / 천잔술
106 / 꽃웃음
108 / 사모 3
110 / 풀벌레
112 / 아버지의 눈
115 / 섬
116 / 몽화
120 / 한라들꽃
122 / 죽심
124 / 가을 나그네
126 / 가을 편지 속을
터는 밤인데
132 / 설야
134 / 장군의 귀환
139 / 군화

144 / 동백꽃 이름으로
살으셨습니다
150 / 포은 선생 최후를
느끼며
152 / 미궁
156 / 녹슨 눈물
158 / 어머니
160 / YK에게
162 / 홍우렁이
164 / 먼 길
166 / 별
168 / 인생만곡
171 / 꽃비에 바다가
그립다
174 / 모진 날이 지나고
176 / 양산 속의 여인
178 / 낮달맞이꽃
180 / 혼적

5부 정낭의 빗장을 풀며

184 / 어부의 아들
188 / 바람의 강
192 / 눈물
194 / 물 허벅질 하는 아이
197 / 정낭의 빗장을 풀며
202 / 몽정
205 / 세월에 논하여
208 / 신세
210 / 밤길에서
212 / 밤비
214 / 바닷길
216 / 젖가슴
218 / 할머니의 버스
222 / 한림 바당
226 / 새벽이여
228 / 성산 일출봉
230 / 호미
234 / 제주의 오름
236 / 의군의 총
244 / 청춘에게

1부 빈집
empty House

인연(因緣)

글자 하나 바뀌었는데
詩가 참, 너그럽다

사람도
좋은 마음을 나눈다면
그러리라

아마도
삶의 멍울도 더러 풀리지 않을까

사랑 또한 노을처럼 익어갈 것이고
참, 너그럽다는 말
언젠가 당신에게 꼭 들었으면
그것이 바람이다

Ties(인연)

One letter has changed.
poim is very generous

People
If you share a good heart
So it will be

Maybe
I wonder if some of the bruises of life will be solved

Love will also ripen like a sunset,
Oh, that's a generous word.
I hope you hear it someday.
That is the desire

동백화(冬栢花)

천 년이 모랫재로 흘러갔어도
이 세상에 때 묻지 않은 꽃

절절한 냉기 속에
꽃봉오리 터지는 통증을 내색하지 않고
스스로 향기를 모두어 피고 피어
오로지 순정 하나로
만개한 검붉은 연정(戀情)

피로 뿌리며 낙화하는 날
그리하여 완전한 절명을 사랑이라 품는

동백화(冬栢花)
붉게 더 붉게 목숨을 사른다

Camellia (동백화)

Even if a thousand years have passed by in the ashes
An unspoiled flower in this world

In the desperate chill
Without expressing the pain of bursting flower buds
Bloom and bloom all the fragrance by yourself
A dark red coalition in full bloom with only one pure spirit

A day sprinkled with blood and falling
Thus the perfect despair is called love.

Camellia (冬栢花)
The redder the redder the life

제주 사람마다 안중의 바람꽃

억센 바람이 분다
기억이 우엉밭을 스치는
소리
낯설지 않다
아
가끔 나는
잔소름으로 돋는 바람에
산다는 일이 소중해져
소리 닿는 어디서
가슴이 이리 간절해 오는
제주 바람
절절한 마음으로
선 채 바람꽃을 피운다
'어디 갔다가 이제서 왔니?'
물어오는
멀리에서 살아가도
지척(咫尺)에 있는 듯 일렁이며
모든 얼굴을 불러
기억으로 다시 사는
아
제주 그 바람꽃

Everyone in Jeju cares about windflowers

The wind blows a strong
Memories flash
through the burdock field
Sound
It's not strange
Ah
Sometimes I
with goosebumps
Life becomes precious
somewhere within the reach
My heart is so desperate
Jeju Wind
with a desperate heart
stand in the wind
'Where have you been and now
where are you from?' Asks
Even if ours live far away
on the edge of one's death
Call all the faces
living again with memory
Ah
The windflowers in Jeju

기억의 등(燈)을 밝히는 말

1편

기억보다 더 짙어진 어둠 속에서는
알 수가 없어
그리움의 고지서
틈 사이 거무스름 물때로 끼고
마음의 문고리는 먼지로 쌓여
켜켜이 불을 끊었는지

다녀간 인연들 어디 살다 떠나는지
두리번거리며 눈질만 바쁜
회억의 자명종, 아련한 음성
기억 끝의 잔말
통발에 걸린 은어(隱語)로 붙든
나

2편

그리움의 배는 늘 먼저 사라져
홀로 항구를 지키는 남겨진 몫
사랑에 겨웠던 사람은 멀리 보내는 것
기억을 숨기지 못하는 유일한 오점은
스스로 풀 수 없던 물음표로 남는다

기억이라는 것이 슬프구나
기억을 잃어버리는 것은
서럽고 서럽구나

삶의 언덕 모든 곳은 가팔라도
꽃이 신록이 화사히 피고
단풍이 물들고 곱던 날에
흰 눈이 오던 날에
인연에 끌려 기억을 나눈 모든 날이

3편

바람이 옷깃을 밀어내면 다시
세상은 지구 밖에서 돌아
가장자리에 유난히 회오리 돌아

이 오랜 기억의 방 두둑히
당신이라고 소롯 앉혀두고
더는 지워지지 않게
다시는 잊혀지지 않게

오늘도 내 먼 안부는
기억의 등이라는
이름을 밝힌다에

Words that light up memories
(기억의 등(燈)을 밝히는 말)

1.

In the darkness that's deeper than I remember
I don't know
a bill of longing
I put it on during the break
The doorway of the heart is covered with dust
Turn it on. Turn it off

The relationships you've been to
where do you live and leave
busy looking around
a nostalgic alarm recollection
the last words of memory
Whether it's a catchy slang
Only I

2.

The belly of longing always disappears
firstthe leftovers of guarding the harbor
alone
If you were in love, send it away
The only stain that can't hide my memory is
It remains a question mark that I couldn't
solve on my own

Memories are sad
Losing your memory is
It's sad and sad

The hills of life, everywhere is a steeple
with bright green flowers
On a day when the autumn leaves
were turning red
on a snowy day
All the days we shared our memories with
each other because of course

3.

When the wind pushes the collar
The world revolves outside the earth
There's an exceptional whirlwind

This room of old memories
I'll let you sit down
So that it doesn't erase anymore
So that I won't forget it again

Today, my distant regards
It's the back of memory
reveal one's name

그 비

흙은 강물에 휩싸여가더니
향기를 잃은 나무는
밤새 신음을 하였다

코끝에 아카시아 향기는
이 땅 위에 점점 아득해졌다

*백석 시인의 시 '비'를 읽고

The Rain (그 비)

The soil was swept away by the river.
A tree that has lost its fragrance
I moaned all night

The scent of acacia on the tip of the nose
It became more and more distant on this earth

*Read the poem 'Rain' by Baek seok Poet

가얏고

한 곡절 다 뜯지도 못하고 농현 소리만
허공 귓전에 맴돈 말들 손가락 끝에서 저리건만
초로(草露)에 불구 하는 이 가슴을 자꾸 흔들어 놓는다

백두 천지로 골짜기 굽이 따라
강물이 흐르는
저 바다는 얼마나 깊고 넓어 검푸르건만
열두 명주실에 매인 운명(運命) 어우르며 사는 삶이런다

소리 울림만으론 이 가락에 잇대지 못하여
깊어진 사정 끊을 도리도 가락이런만
한 생애(生涯)를 이끈 가슴은 뜬 달만큼 처연히 외로웁다

Gayatgo(가얏고)

I can't even tear off a whole circumference, only the sound of the strings
The words in the air, the words that hover in my ears, the fingertips that go from the tips of my fingers to the elderly, keep shaking this chest in spite of the elderly

Along the bend of the valley to the Paektu Heaven and Earth
The river flows
How deep and wide is that sea
It is a life lived in harmony with fate, bound by twelve silk threads

The sound alone is not enough to connect with this rhythm.
Even if you can't stop the deepened ejaculation, you can only do it
The heart that has led a lifetime is as lonely as the moon

둘이서 가까이하고픈 까닭은

둘이서 가까이하고픈 까닭은
서로 알뜰히 살펴주는 일이다
한 사람이 힘겨워할 때
꼭 손을 놓지 말고 이끌어주는 일이다

사실 사랑한다는 말을 더듬어도
그 마음에 미소를 짓게 하는 일이다
삶의 고달픔에도 기댈 수 있도록
사뭇 어깨를 내어 토닥이는 일이다

작은 식탁에 담긴 정성 가득히
오붓한 일상의 맛을 누리는 일이다
가끔 추억의 풍경을 뒤적이곤
공감을 나누며 여생을 닮아가는 일이다

꽃향기 폴폴나는 꽃길을 걷듯이
머리 위에 웃음꽃이 만연히 피는 일이다
산등성이에 석양을 지켜보며
아름답게 익어가고픈 일이다

밤하늘에 뜬 별을 동경하듯이
사랑을 지피며 어울리는 일이다
둘이서 가까이하고픈 까닭은
새 아침에 함께 눈을 뜨는 일이다

The reason why you two want to be close to each other 둘이서 가까
이하고픈 까닭은

 The reason why you two want to be close to each other It's about taking
care of each other
When One Person Is Struggling
It's a matter of guiding them without letting go

In fact, even if you stutter to say that you love me
It's something that brings a smile to your face
So that we can lean on the hardships of life
It's a pat on the shoulder

Filled with care at a small table
It's about enjoying the taste of everyday life
Sometimes I rummage through the scenery of memories It's about sharing
empathy and becoming like the rest of your life

The fragrance of flowers is like walking on a path of flowers Laughter blooms
overhead.
Watching the sunset on the ridge
It's something that I want to ripen beautifully

Like longing for the stars in the night sky
It's about making love and hanging out
The reason why the two of you want to be close to each other
It's about waking up together in a new morning

첫 연가

아름다운 이여
부디 용서하시오
잠시 나 그댈 잊었으니

그리움이 깨는 이 아침
오는 숨소리에
일찍 깨어 마중하리니

어서 오시오
기쁨이고 반가움인
그대를 맞이하면

눈물은 거짓말처럼 마르고
모든 슬픔은 지워져

아름다운 이여
항상 내 마음 청춘에 젖어
끝이나 처음인 사랑을
노래로 노래 부를 것이니

First stanza (첫연가)

Beautiful Lady,
Please forgive me
I've forgotten about it for a while.

This morning when nostalgia awakens
To the sound of the coming breath
I will wake up early and meet you.

Welcome.
It's a joy and a pleasure
When I greet you,

Tears dry like a lie,
All sorrow is erased

Beautiful Lady,
Always immersed in the youth of my heart
Love that is the end or the beginning
I will sing with song.

고독(孤獨)

모든 사람이 잠든 이 밤에
소리 내어 웃는 자가 나요
울고 있는 자가 또한 나외다

난 누구에게로
그대들은 또한 어디론가로
그리움의 불씨를 날리고

모든 사람이 잠든 이 밤에
한때의 청춘으로
흰 여백에 고독(孤獨)을 처절히 쓰고 있다

Solitude(고독)

On this night when everyone was asleep
Someone laughs out loud
I am also the one who weeps

Who am I to
You also go somewhere
Blowing the embers of longing

On this night when everyone was asleep
As a youth once
Solitude is written in the white space

청보리 소리

사월이면 아이는
들판으로 무작정 나갑니다
하늘 바람이 불면 사르르
양쪽 귓불을
노래하듯 간지럽히고
호미질하는
어머니의 허리는 굽어가고
청보리 소리에
아이는 그만 잠이 듭니다

사월이면 아이는
들판으로 무작정 나갑니다
하늘 바람이 불면 사르르
춤을 추며 초록 물결처럼 살랑대고
어머니의 호미질에
햇볕에 누렇게 익어가고
청보리 소리에
아이는 그만 잠이 듭니다

The sound of green barley(청보리 소리)

If it's April, the child will
Blindly go out into the field
When the sky wind blows
Sarr
Both earlobes
Tickle like a song,
Homizing
My mother's waist is bent,
To the sound of green barley
The child is
Stop falling asleep

If it's April, the child will
Blindly go out into the field
When the sky wind blows
Sarr
Dancing
Fluttering like a green wave
To my mother's homie
The sun is ripening yellow,
To the sound of green barley
The child is
Stop falling asleep

향수병(鄕愁病)

바람이 제일 거친 곳을 골라 연을 날린다
더 멀리 애절한 그곳으로 남아 있는 이름들 바닥을 긁어 바
람에 맡긴다
가까이 있던 일들 빨리 잊어가고
허망한 욕심은 겨울 왕벚나무처럼 가지만 남아 잃어버린 그
것만 남겨진 세상
현실을 다 벗은 나 혼자 나르는 중이다
내일을 알지 못했던 그것은 두려움과 자유와 몽환이었던 곳
한낱 손바닥으로 세상을 가린 아이였던 날 뛰어놀던 동백꽃
동산과
높고 흰 산 아래 붉은 지붕의 집들과 가장 파릇한 바다와
풍금 소리 들려오던 학교와 일선 애순 희자 지훈이 동네 아
이들의 이름과
모든 것들은 그 자리에서 자라고 있겠지
혼자 떨어진 나도 거기 함께 있겠지
잘라버린 연줄에 매달린 나의 연이
곳자왈 숲우듬지에 이어져 여태 낮은 숨을 쉬었는데 줄 없
는 연을 날린다
바람이 제일 많은 곳 누구도 찾지 못하는 '곳'에서 내게서
점점 잊히려 한다

Homesickness(향수병)

Pick a place where the wind is the toughest and fly a kite
Names that remain in a mournful place farther away,
scraping the floor and leaving it to the wind
Quickly forget the things that were close to you,
Vain greed goes like a cherry tree in winter, but it is left
and lost.
I'm carrying it all by myself
It was not known tomorrow
A place of fear, freedom, and dreams
The day I was a child who covered the world with a mere
palm
The camellia garden where I used to play
Under the high white mountains, the red-roofed houses,
the bluest sea, and the sound of the wind
School and front-line ilsun Aesoon Hee-ja Jihoon The
names of the children in the neighborhood and
Everything is growing on its spot
I'll be there with you, even if I'm alone
My kite hanging from a severed kite rope
Leading up to the forest of gokjJawal, I have been breathing
low so far, but I fly a kite without a rope
In the windiest place, the "cape" where no one can find it,
it is about to be forgotten by me more and more

고향의 서(序)

나는
광화문에 가면 그의 시를 쓴다
서대문에 가면 그의 시를 쓴다

그냥 지나쳐온 나는
어디에 있는 걸까 하면

아버지가 서 있는
고향

나 거기에 있기나 한 것일까

a writing of Hometown(고향의 서)

I am
When I go to Gwanghwamun, I write his poems
When I go to Seodaemun, I write his poems

I've just walked past
Where is it

Father standing
hometown

Am I there

국화꽃 향기 앞에서

산 이름을 묻지 마라
강 이름도 묻지 마라
이 땅을 밟고 가는 이들이여
마치 고귀한 영혼은 침묵하듯이
들판엔 국화가 하얀 향기를 조용히 흔든다

푸른 하늘에는
솔개가 옛 영광을 찾아 자유로이 활개를 친다

산은 살아있다
강은 살아있다
이 땅에 살아가는 이들이여
얼마나 눈부시게 아름다운 곳이란 말이던가

해는 솟아오르고
높은 산에 우러르러 산양이 지키고 있고
깊은 골짜기에
젖 줄기 같은 강이 끊임없이 흐른다

조국을 위하여
청춘을 위하여
그 산과 강에 고요히 잠든 선열(先烈)을 위하여
이 땅의 들판을 거닐 때면
언제나 국화가 피어나
하얀 향기를 조용히 흔든다
국화꽃 향기 앞에서

In front of the fragrance
of chrysanthemum flowers(국화꽃 향기 앞에서)

Don't ask for the name of the mountain
Don't even ask for the name of the river
Those who tread on this earth,
As if the noble soul is silent
In the fields, chrysanthemums quietly shake their white
fragrance

In the blue sky
The pine dog roars freely in search of its former glory

The mountains are alive
The river is alive
Those who live on this earth,
What a dazzlingly beautiful place

The sun is rising,
The high mountains are guarded by mountain goats,
In the deep valley
A milk-like river flows incessantly

For the sake of the motherland
For the sake of youth
For the glandular fever that sleeps quietly in the mountains
and rivers

When you walk through the fields of this land
Chrysanthemums always bloom
Shake the white fragrance quietly
In   front   of   the   fragrance   of   chrysanthemum
flowersLiberation Day

If you were responsible for
your work yesterday
I am responsible for all my work today.
I will do it

광복(光復)의 날

어제
당신의 그 일에 책임(責任)을 지셨다면
나는 오늘 나의 모든 일에 책임(責任)을
다할 것입니다

Liberation Day (광복의 날)

If you were responsible for your
work yesterday
I am responsible for all my work today.
I will do it

이시돌 성당

빈집

그 집에는 지금 아무도 없다

몇 해 전만 해도
당신의 성성한 모습 생생한 목소리
큰길 건너에까지 들리고도 남아

집 안팎에 아른거리는 모습들이
생애 온 마음 쥐어 짜낸 슬픔일까
담아두었던 많은 말이 들고 난 정이
와르르 쏟아져 마당에 흥건한데

돌담 화단에
가지런히 동백꽃 분분히 떨어지고
오래 묵은 귤나무에도 빈 가지만 남아
철철 넘치던 물소리 끊긴 수북한 먼지뿐인
낡은 수돗가에 서서
허옇게 허옇게 색이 바랜 지붕 아래
창문틀 가까이 키득대던
아이의 웃음도

모든 것이 옛것이다
기억만이 힘겨운 마중이다

낡은 여닫이문 비식 열리며
내 이름을 부를 것만 같은 당신
죽음 너머에서도
기다릴 것만 같은 모습 선연해

탱자 가시에 생살 찢겨나는 듯 쓰라린데
몇 날을 지새워도 치유되지 못할 얼굴들과
당신이 누운 그 자리 세미소 오름 위
흰 구름이 하염없이 내려다뵈는 빈집

그 빈집으로 봄은 오고 있는 것일까

empty house (빈집)

There is no one in the house now

A few years ago,
Your Holy Figure, Your Vivid Voice
Even across the main road it remains

I've never seen them flirting around the house
Is it the sadness that I squeezed out of my whole life
I kept a lot of things in my mind
I'm filled with affection
It's in the yard

With a faded roof
Struggling close to the window frame
The kid's smile
Everything's old

Memory is the only way to greet you
The old hinged door opens
You who will call my name
beyond death
I'll show you how I'll be waiting for you

Bitter like a bone in a tangja

Even if I stay up for a few days, I'll be able to see the rest

of my face

The place where you lie down

Still on top of semisso

an empty house overlooking white clouds

Is spring coming to the empty house

채당

눈 오는 밤에

2부 천 걸음

A Thousand Steps

세미소 오름길

사모 1

세미소 오름에 바람은 모질게도 궂습니다

사모하는 그리운 임이여
세월이 야속하니
소리를 잃은 눈물은 가슴으로 나립니다

붉은 흙 덮인 금빛 잔디는
초록빛으로 돋아 언제 푸른 기운일지
못난 자식은 사뭇 걱정을 드리웁니다

구름은 흘러서 떠나가듯이
다시 올 날 선뜻 기약하지 못합니다

베푸셨던 온 정 가슴으로 지피며
아무 데서나 또 눈물을 짓지 않으렵니다

dear 1 (사모 1)

The wind is brutally bad at Semiso oreum

I miss you dearly
The years are savage
Tears that have lost their voice fall in my heart

The golden grass covered with red soil
It sprouts green, when will it become blue?
Poor children cause great anxiety.

As the clouds flow and leave
I can't promise the day I'll come again

The warmth you gave me blooms in her heart
I won't shed tears anywhere again

바다를 끓이다

바다에 건져 올린 그리움을
해풍에 말린다

뜨거운 햇살에 드러누워
바닥 위에 검게 익어가고
굳은살에 박힌 등줄기는 식은땀이 흐른다

차곡차곡 쌓인 세간에
한 생의 일부를 꺼내놓고는
자글자글 끓는 물에 한 조각씩 떼어낸다

어머니는 산후에 미역국 한 그릇 안
세상을 일평생 읽는다

Boil the sea(바다를 끓이다)

The longing that was lifted up to the sea
It is dried by the sea breeze

Lying naked in the hot sun
Ripening black on the bottom,
A cold sweat flows down the back of the callus

In the world that has accumulated one by one
Pulling out a part of a life,
Peel off each piece in boiling water

My mother has a bowl of seaweed soup after giving birth
Read the world for the rest of your life

유산(遺産)

내가 물려받은 것은
오로지 사랑이란
근간(根幹)이다

heritage 유산

what I inherited
is only love
is the root

한라산 철쭉꽃

거대한 산

난 굴곡진 길을
일생 오르내렸다

저만치
산 하나가
보였다

가까이 가보니
나의 앞길에
풍상(風霜)을 막아주고 있다

그것은
거대한 산

Huge mountain (거대한 산)

I'm on a winding road
A lifetime of ups and downs

Far away
One mountain
Looked

As I got closer,
On my way
It prevents wind damage

That's
Huge mountain

아버지의 기억

어선이 귀지근한 바닷가에 닻 내리고 어린 담장 안
가지 끝에 잡어들이 허공 위 기억을 더듬는다

고단한 하루 밀물에 헹구어 가던 길 한림항에 날이 저물어가면 파
도 소리에 소라를 끓이는 할머니의 분주함에 자리가 채워지고 아
버지의 바다에 절었던 파릇한 입술처럼 술잔 안에 물결이 출렁이
듯 파전과 고들빼기에 하루를 마신다

그물처럼 엮어지고 짭조름한 바람이 검버섯에 주름진 아버지의 얼
굴이 가득 찬 술잔에 놓이는 그리움은 끝없이 깊고 깊어지더니 어
둑해져 뭍으로 돌아오는 길은 자전거 뒤 짐칸에 희망을 싣고 돌밭
길로 달리시던 아버지의 땀 냄새가 흠뻑 밴 그 등이 한라산 백록
담처럼 높고 또 깊어만 보였다

유년은 술잔 안에 담겨서 차가운 가슴은 뜨겁게 눈물에 데워지고
세월에 절인 아버지의 젖은 심장을 수평선 너머 노을 끝에 하염없
이 말린다

Memories of my father (아버지의 기억)

On the shore where the fishing boat is cute
Anchored and young inside the fence
At the end of the branches, the fish grope for memories in
the air

On a hard day, when the day comes to an end at the port
of Hallim, the sound of the waves fills the place with the
bustle of the grandmother boiling the conch, and like the
blue lips that bowed in the sea of my father, the waves in
the glass of wine ripple and drink the day

The longing that was woven like a net, and the salty wind
rested on the drinking cup full of my father's wrinkled face
with age spots, was endlessly deep and deep, and when it
got dark and the way back to the shore was drenched with
the smell of my father's sweat as he rode on the stony
road with hope in the luggage compartment behind his
bicycle, his back seemed as high and deep as the white
green wall of Halla Mountain

Childhood is placed in a drinking cup, and the cold chest
is heated with hot tears, and the wet heart of the father,
marinated in time, is dried at the end of the sunset over
the horizon

한라산 편지

지금 나는 몹시 그립다
아주 오래전 마음의 빗장을 여는 편지를 쓴다

깊은 밤을 절제할 수 없는 젊은 날의 고독처럼
또 하나의 그리움에 흰 산이 드높게만 보였다

그 어떤 노래로 진정할 수 없고
상심의 바다에 구하지 못하는 가슴이 뜨겁다

어둠에서 빛들은 한산하고 적요하여
잊었던 이름 가슴에 다가와 별처럼
동백나무는 돌담 집을 지키고
누이는 고단한 삶의 기도로 뒤척이는 밤
아직도 나는 별을 헤며 산다

온갖 두려움이 덜어지기를
혼잣말로 주절인다

누이가 선잠에서 놀라 깨어나지 않도록
남아 있는 일은 나의 기도
여백의 미지를 붙잡고 먼저 생각에 잠긴다

억센 바람이 진눈깨비 몰고 오는 날
한라산 철쭉나무가 폭설에 묻히는 소식

누이가 감기에 혹여 걸리지 않을까
두려움이 가리는 그곳으로 함께 있기를
홀로 있는 외로움을 잔설처럼
털어내고 있다

수평선에서 해가 산을 들어 올리면
파란 지붕 너머 옥빛 바다로 스러지고
밤은 지난 일의 상처를 씻듯 별을 닦는다

나는 가슴 떨리는 이 향수가 밀감처럼
익어가고
한라산 백록담에 올라 볼 수 없는
생각 한 자락에
성산 앞바다의 일출을 가슴에 실컷 품는다

Hallasan Letter (한라산 편지)

Now I miss it terribly
A long time ago, I write a letter that opens the bars of my heart

Like the solitude of a young day when you can't control the deep night
In another nostalgia, the white mountains loomed high

I can't calm down with any song.
The heart that cannot be saved by the sea of heartache is hot

In the darkness the lights are still and still,
A forgotten name comes to your chest like a star
Camellias guard the stone-walled house,
My sister tosses and turns in the prayers of a hard life
Still I live in the stars

May all fears be alleviated.
I sobbed to myself

So that your sister doesn't wake up from her slumber
All that remains is my prayer
Grasp the unknown in the margins and think about it first

A day when a strong wind brings sleet
News of Hallasan azaleas being buried in heavy snow

I wonder if my sister will catch a cold
Be with us where fear obscures us
The loneliness of being alone
I'm brushing it off

When the sun lifts the mountains from the horizon
Beyond the blue roof to the jade sea,
The night wipes the stars as if to wash the wounds of the past

I feel that this perfume that trembles in my heart ripens like wheat,
You can't climb the White Rock Wall of Halla Mountain
At the edge of my mind
Embrace the sunrise off the coast of Seongsan in your heart

그냥

비가 내려
자꾸 비가 내린다
길가에 아이는 비닐우산을 쓴 체
검정 짧은 바지에 파란 장화를 신은 두 발로
멜로디 없이도
그냥 노래처럼 첨벙거린다

비가 내려
자꾸 비가 내린다
길가에 엄마는 우산 하나 없는 체
이름 모를 작은 꽃과 초록 나무와 나란히 젖어도
희망을 읽듯이
그냥 시처럼 낭만이 보인다

just

It's raining
It's raining all the time
On the side of the road, a child wears a plastic umbrella
With two feet in black short pants and blue boots
Even without a melody
It just splashes like a song

It's raining
It's raining all the time
On the side of the road, my mom doesn't have an umbrella
Even if I get wet side by side with a nameless small flower and
a green tree
As if reading hope
It just looks romantic, like a poem

공양(供養)

어머니 부엌에
밥상이 차려진다

물기 묻은 손이
긁히고
데이고
갈라지고

평생을 보살처럼
살아왔다

Gongyang (供養)

mother in the kitchen
the table is set

wet hands
scratched
deigo
Cracked

Like taking care of she whole life
have lived

천 걸음

귀또리가 우는 가슴이 물든 밤입니다

비좁은 도시 가로등 불빛 따라
그림자 홀로 휘적대고 있습니다

철 지난 장미 넝쿨이 담벼락을 넘어
보다 붉게 태우는 마지막 향연이
초라해 보입니다

낯선 이곳을 익숙히 지나갈 적에
습관처럼 내 눈에 먼지가
자꾸만 끼어듭니다

흰 눈이 쌓인 산과
파도가 밀려오던 푸른 바다가
외로운 달빛에
유년의 기억이 비춰들었습니다

당신의 울타리 안에 있던 날
솜이불처럼 포근하기만 한데
지금 아무리 걸어도 갈 수 없는 그곳은
천 걸음 만큼
저 멀리에 떨어져 아득합니다

어머니, 이 밤에 불빛을 등지고
빛나는 별 하나 나는 바라만 보고 있습니다

A thousand steps (천 걸음)

It's a heart-wrenching night when crickets cry

Along the light of the cramped city street lamps
Shadows are swirling alone

Season-long rose vines over the wall
The last feast that burns redder
It looks shabby

When you pass by a strange place,
Dust in my eyes, like a habit
I keep interrupting

Mountains covered with white snow
The blue sea where the waves came
In the lonely moonlight
Childhood memories came flooding back

The Day I Was Inside Your Fence
It's as cozy as a cotton quilt
No matter how much you walk now, you can't go to that place
As much as a thousand steps
It's far away

Mother, turn your back on the lights this night
A shining star, I can only look at it

바다가 웃는다

바다가 웃는다
나도 따라 웃는다

바다가 웃는다
나도 배시시 웃는다

바다가
내 까만 눈물을
다 용서하고,

바다가 덩실댄다
나도 얼싸안고 춤을 추었다

The sea smile (바다가 웃는다)

The sea smile
I smile along too

The sea smile
I smile at the cute too

Sea
My black tears
Forgive all,

The sea is roaring
I hugged and danced too

독백(獨白)

참 슬프기도 합니다
어쩌면 세상이 제 원대로 돌지 않습니다

무성한 나무의 잎새가 지고는
앙상한 가지만 처연히 드러낸다 하여도
자연의 이치에 상생하는 관계입니다

구르는 돌멩이가 제 자리를 잡고
뒹구는 낙엽조차 가지런히 모여 있는데
바람같이 존재 없는 나는
거친 숨 고르기가 버거운 이유는 무엇입니까

누이의 빈 자리를 외로이 서성이다가
한동안 눈물샘마저 다 치르고 나면
그다음 타버린 심장이 멎을 것만 같습니다

나 이제 알았습니다
젊은 날의 웃음이 잊을 것 같은 두려움에
뜬 달이 기울어질 때까지
그 마음의 공백에 어지러이 돌고 돌았습니다

헤어지고 난 뒤에 빛을 잃어버린 자리
얼마나 중한지 뼈아프게 몸으로 읽혀 듭니다
여태 새겨둔 마음을 써 내려 갈 수 있으면
밤 서리에 젖어도 그 슬픔까지
난 수긍하겠습니다

Monologue 독백

True It's sad
Maybe the world doesn't turn the way I want it to

The leaves of the lush trees are falling,
The tree only bare its delicate branches,
It is a win-win relationship according to the principles of nature

The rolling stones are in place,
Even the fallen leaves are neatly clustered,
I am as non-existent as the wind
Why is it hard to catch your breath?

Pacing lonely in his sister's empty seat,
After a while of exhausting the tear ducts,
And then my burned heart seems to stop

I know now
In the fear that the laughter of a young day will be forgotten
Until the moon rises and tilts
I dizzily turned and spun in that mental void

A place that has lost its shine after a breakup
I read how serious it is.
If you can write down the heart that you have carved so far
Even if you get wet with the night frost, even the sadness
I'll accept

아름다운 날에

화사한 봄의 아침
푸른 하늘가 긴 여정에 머무르는
나는 구름입니다

진달래꽃으로 단장한 산에
그리움 깊은 마음으로 흔들리는
나는 바람입니다

해맑은 호수 같은 고운 누이여
긴 머리의 동백꽃 향기에 흠뻑 취해버린
나는 나무입니다

저 멀리 내다보는 바닷가에 은빛 포말을 일으키고
이내 스러져가는 가슴 앓은
나는 파도입니다

나는 구름이고
나는 바람이며
나는 나무와 나는 파도가 되었습니다

그리하여 난 누이에게
그 이름으로 기억되고 싶은 존재입니다

On a beautiful day 아름다운 날에

Bright Spring Morning
The blue sky lingers on the long journey
I am a cloud

On the mountain adorned with rhododendron flowers
Nostalgia shakes with a deep heart
I am the wind

A fair sister like a clear lake,
Drunk with the scent of camellias with long hair
I am a tree

Raising a silver foam on the distant seashore,
Heartburn that soon fades
I am a wave

I am a cloud,
I am the wind,
I became a tree and I became a wave

So I said to my sister,
I want to be remembered by that name

비의 회억

매지 구름 한올 두올 바람으로 깁던 날
낮달은 돌아올 줄 모르고
아버지의 술 오른 고함만
천둥소리보다 무섭게
하늘을 내려 앉히고 있다
쥐 눈을 한 아이는
할머니의 젖가슴에서
별이 뜨기만을 기다리다
장대비가 어둠을 갈기갈기
찢는 소리를 들으며
쥐 눈을 한 아이가 할머니 품속에서
허기진 배를 채우고 돌아갈 때면
말간 하늘은 쥐 눈 같은 별들을 박고 있다

Rain revolving 비의 회억

A day when the clouds of Madge were covered with a breeze
The day moon does not know how to return,
Only my father's drunken yelling
Scarier than thunder
It's letting the sky go down
The child with the mouse eye
From my grandmother's breasts
Waiting for the Stars to Rise
The pole grinds the darkness
Listening to the sound of tearing
A mouse-eyed child in her grandmother's arms
When I go home with a full stomach
The sky is studded with stars like rat eyes

사모 2

구름을 밀어내고 달빛이 다가옵니다
풀 향기 길을 따라 당신이 사무쳐서
봄날을 묵란 한 송이에 사랑이라 적습니다

dear 2 (사모 2)

Push away the clouds and
the moonlight approaches
The scent of grass along the way you are soaked
Write the word love in a bunch of spring

춘천물 폭나무

사랑을 위하여,
잠 못 이루는 벗에게

수많은 밤 그토록 별을 헤아리는 까닭은
기다릴 사람조차 있는 것도 아니지만
깊어만 갈수록 오랜 기억을 헤매이기에
갈바람 잎새 위에 먹빛을 흩날리오

지난 스물하고도 한 살이 되던 해
사랑의 상처를 더듬거리며
어느 가난한 로망스의 시인처럼
잠 못 이루어 홀로 지샜던 연고의 밤

하얀 천 속에 간직한 빛바랜 사진 한 장
그리고 때 묻은 바이런 시집을 펼쳐보노라면
비록 먼 곳에 가 없는 사랑일지라도
내 한 가슴 속에 숨 쉬고 있어라

젊은 날의 벗이여!
남은 시간을 위하여
모든 사람들을 사랑해다오

지난 스물하고도 한 살이 되던 해
사랑의 아픔 때문에 괴로워하던
잠 못 이루어 지샌 그 밤은 너무도 아름다웠소

*G.G 로드 바이런: 영국 낭만파 시인, 철학가
*1986년 가을에 쓴 詩

For love's sake,
To a Sleepless Friend

Why do we count so many stars on so many nights
It's not like there's even anyone to wait for.
The deeper I go, the more I wander through my old memories
Scatter the ink on the leaves of the wind,

When I was twenty-one years old,
Stuttering through the wounds of love
Like a poor poet of romance
A sleepless night of solitude

A faded photograph in a white cloth
And as I open the stained collection of Byron's poems,
Even if it is a love that is far away,
Breathe in my heart

Friend of the young days!
For the rest of your time
Love all people

When I was twenty-one years old,
Troubled by the Pain of Love
That sleepless night was so beautiful

*G.G. Lord Byron, English Romantic poet and philosopher
*Written in the fall of 1986

올래길 집 앞

가을의 기도

가을입니다
낙엽들이 거리에 나뒹굴고
혼자 있는 것으로 고독합니다
할애받은 시간 중에
삶에 허덕이는 나의 존재를 깨우치고
기도하게 하소서

완연한 가을입니다
죄는 미워해도 사람은 용서하듯이
용기를 잃지 않게 해주십시오
모든 이와 함께하며
또 다른 삶으로 나의 모습을 보이고
사랑하게 하소서

A Pray of Autumn　가을의 기도

It's autumn
Leaves are scattered on the street
I'm lonely being alone
during the allotted time
Awakening to my existence struggling with life
let me pray

Autumn is in full swing
Just as people forgive sins even though they hate them
Please do not lose courage
with everyone
show me in another life
let me love you

무궁화

언제나 피어 있습니다

이 가슴에
지지 않은 꽃

당신입니다

mugungwha 무궁화

It's always in bloom

In this chest
Unsung flowers

It's you

장 속의 새

아직 눈이 뜨이지 않은, 안개 속의 나

별을 더듬는 나를 찾는다

수많은 나날을 멋을 찾는 방랑자처럼

온 세상을 보기 위하여 온갖 몸짓을 하며 말한다

푸른 창공을 날기 위하여

장 속에 갇힌 새는 구슬피 울어댄다

그리고 나는 시인이 되기 위하여

이 밤도 별을 찾아 헤메인다

그래서 자연을 찾아 갈구하며

그들과 얘기하고 한참 나를 찾는 중이다

눈이 뜨이면 눈이 부시도록 넓은 세상으로 나에게

역시 장 속의 풀려난 새는

하늘을 마음껏 날아다닐 것이다

나는 시인이 되기 위하여

이 밤도 별을 더듬는 나를 찾는다

3부 한라아리랑

Halla Arirang

한라아리랑

아리 아리 아리랑 한라- 아리 아리랑
한이 눈물 된 바다
한숨이 쌓인 한라산
아리랑 아리랑 아리랑 아리랑
이제 가면 언제 오나 한라-아-리랑

아리 아리 아리랑 한라- 아리 아리랑
시련은- 큰바위
설움은 작은 모래알
아리랑 아리랑 아리랑 아리랑
이제 가면 언제 오나 한라- 아-리랑

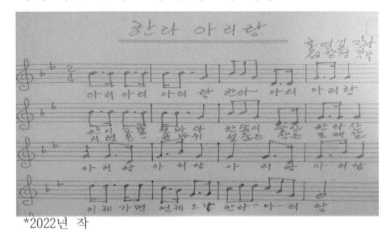

*2022년 작

Halla Arirang 한라아리랑

Ari Ari Arirang Halla- Ari Arirang
Han is a sea of tears
Hallasan where sighs pile up
Arirang Arirang Arirang Arirang
If you go now,
when will you come, Halla-ah-Lirang

Ari Ari Arirang Halla- Ari Arirang
The ordeal is- The Big Rock
Sadness is a small grain of sand
Arirang Arirang Arirang Arirang
If you go now,
when will you come, Halla-ah-Lirang

죽도록 지독한 이별의 사랑은

꽃이 죽고
나무도 죽고
산도 새까맣게 타 죽었습니다
메마른 강물은 쪼들어가고
바다로 흘러갈 여력조차 없습니다
이제 하늘 위에는
해마저 먹구름으로 가려졌습니다

별은 죽고
바람도 죽고
詩가 시들어서 막 죽었습니다
죽도록 지독한 이별의 사랑은
뜨거운 눈물을 흘릴 여분도 없습니다
푸른 기억이 빠져버린 춘천물에
한 사나이의 계절은 잃어버렸습니다

*춘천물: 상명里. 빗물못

The love of parting,
which is terrible to death 죽도록

The flower dies,
The tree also dies,
The mountains were also burned black to death
The parched rivers are pecked,
They can't even afford to go out to sea
Now above the sky
Even the sun was obscured by dark clouds

The star dies,
The wind dies too,
The poem withered and just died
The love of parting, which is terrible to death,
There is no extra room for hot tears

In the water of Chuncheon
where the blue memories are lost
One man's season is lost

*Chuncheonmul: Sangmyeong里. Rain pond

슬픈 자화상

세상에서 난 가장 가난한 슬픈 자다

이름을 알리려 해도 노래로 부르려 해도
눈물 마른 가슴은 애타고 다문 입은 말 잃어버렸다

걷고 걸어도 당도할 수 없는 이정표 없는 바다 그 한가운데
섬에 사랑을 상실한 마음 아련한 달빛에 출렁인다

*밤의 교향곡에 고조된 음(音)이 향수에 흐르면 꽃의 향기는
가까이 없고 허기진 나비같이 흠뻑 심취한다

그리움의 여력이 궁핍, 애증, 회환, 절망을 느끼는 순간
고독을 탕진해버린 헤어진 속 안에
스스로 모멸에 홀린 자괴감은 형편없이
밀려든다

눈이 멀어도 맨 처음 선명히 떠오르는 것은
슬픔의 치매는 진정 사랑을 찾는다는 병이라

시의 고난이여 묻는다면 답하노니 죽음이 또 나를 갈라놓아
도 긴 밤 위에 목숨 다해 나는 푸른 마음을 새겨놓는다

또한, 그대여 가난한 슬픔을 즐겨라

*밤의 교향곡: 구스타프 말러(1860.7~1911.5)
오스트리아 출생 지휘자, 작곡가
교향곡 7번 (밤의 노래)

Sad Self-Portrait (슬픈 자화상)

I am the poorest sad person in the world

Even if you try to make a name for yourself or sing a song
The tear-soaked chest was anxious, and the words were lost

A sea without a signpost that you can't reach even if you walk
and walk, and in the middle of it, a heart that has lost love on
an island is fluttering in the light of the moon

* When the high-pitched notes of the symphony of the night
flow into the perfume, the fragrance of the flowers is not close
by, but is soaked like a hungry butterfly

The moment when the power of longing makes you feel deprivation, love-hate, remorse, and despair
In the broken up that squandered the solitude
The self-destructive feeling that I shed in self-destruction is terrible
Rush in

Even if you are blind, the first thing that comes to mind clearly is
The dementia of grief is the disease of finding true love.

Afflictions of poetry, if you ask me, I answer, Even if death separates me again, I will engrave a blue heart with all my life on the long night

Also, enjoy your poor sorrows

*Symphony of the Night:
Gustav Mahler (1860.7~1911.5)
Austrian-born conductor and composer
Symphony No. 7 (Song of the Night)

천 잔술

날 샐 때까지
날이 밝을 때부터
시(時) 두지 않고서
마시는 술이다

a thousand glasses 천 잔술

until it leaks me
since the sun rises
without leaving the time
it's a drink

*취중주필, 이규보 노년의 시에서 감상하며

꽃웃음

아이는
꽃을 보고
웃는다

나도
아이처럼
웃는다

Flower smile 꽃웃음

The child is
Looking at the flowers
smile

Me too
Like a child
smile

사모 3

간밤에 다녀가신 당신의 꿈자리에
온기가 따스한 듯 아직도 선명하고
묘지 위 벌초를 한 후 소나기 내립니다

dear 3 (사모 3)

In your dreams that you went to last night
The warmth is still vivid,
After the bee weeding over the graveyard, a rain shower falls

풀벌레

가을밤 깊은데
풀벌레 우네

고향은 산 너머
바닷길은 수백 리

이슬 젖은 옷
마를 새가 없듯이

해 오르는 아침에
풀벌레 우네

Grass beetle 풀벌레

Deep in the autumn night
Grass beetle cry

home is over the mountains
Hundreds of miles of sea

dew wet clothes
As there are no birds to dry

Even in the morning when the sun rises
Grass beetle cry

아버지의 눈

고목 같던 세월의 뿌리 내리느라
모질었던 세상의 파도에 깊은 골옹이를 패며 헤쳐온
아버지

귤나무에 밀감이 익을 때까지
숱한 고생의 피땀은 들에 흘러 흐르고
온몸으로 끌어 바다에 쏟은 일
온몸으로 모아 산 위에 쌓은 업적(業績)

거친 대항에 맞부딪친 삶이
용장(勇將)인 사람

몇 마지기 검은 땅에 돌밭을 캐어 쌓은 일생은 훈장인
근성으로 남아

검푸른 바다를 안고
흰 산을 등에 지고도
그저 웃음만은 잃지 않으시던
아버지

넓고 높은 산에 일구시던 터전은
아버지의 눈 안에 깊어지고
백태로 낀 칡넝쿨 같이 농익었다

흐려진 세상 위로
고목은 초록빛 물감을 뿜어
인생의 풍경을 파랗게 그려놓는다

A Father's Eye 아버지의 눈

Putting down the roots of the old trees
Driven through the waves of a turbulent world,
Father

Until the citrus ripens on the tangerine tree
The blood and sweat of many hardships flow in the field,
What I dragged with my whole body into the sea
Achievements gathered together and built on the mountain

A life confronted with tough opposition
A Man Who Is a Paragon

A lifetime of digging stones into the black ground for a few
miles remained a medal of grit.

Embracing the dark blue sea
Even with the white mountains on your back,
He just smiled.
Father

The home that he built on a wide and high mountain
Deepened in the eyes of the Father,
It was ripe like a white squirt

Above the cloudy world
The old trees spew green paint
Paint the landscape of life in blue

섬

그대의 눈물 고인
바다, 그 자리에
난 베고 누웠습니다

island

Your tears
The sea, in its place
I lay down on my head

몽화(夢花)

그렇게 그리웠다는 말이다
정녕 바윗돌 틈에 꽃을 피우기까지
기다려온 사람이 수고로움을 깨닫듯 절절함은 역력했다
는 말이다

한 사람의 마음도 알아내지 못한 심정은
어떤 말로도 유희할 수 없다
위안거리도 삼을 것이 없는 외로움을 지탱시킨 바램은
그것 역시 하나이고
본심(本心)이다

죽지 못해 사는 것과 살지 못해 죽고 싶은 것 사는 이
유인지 알 수가 없다
달이 뜨고 다시 달이 기울면 모든 사람도 삼라(森羅)도
곤히 잠이 드는 것도 기다리는 일에 지쳐간 심경을 바
라보는
오롯이 그리움인 인생(人生)

기적인 나날,
눈이 부시도록 피어난 하얀 꽃
진정 간밤에 꾸다 진 꿈이어도
사랑할 수밖에 없는 꿈속의 초개(草芥)
하얀 서리 닮은 몽화(夢花)
그립다는 말이 핀 꿈이다

Monghua(夢花)

I mean, I missed him so much
Until it blossoms in the crevices of the rocks
It is said that the desperation was strong, as if the person who
had been waiting realized the hard work

The feeling that I have not been able to grasp even one
person's heart
No words can play
The hope that sustained the loneliness of having nothing to take
as a source of comfort
That, too, is one.
It's true

I don't know if it's because I can't live and I want to die
because I can't live, or if that's why I live
When the moon rises and the moon tilts again, everyone will
also have Samra
Looking at the heart that is tired of waiting for a good sleep
A life of nostalgia

Days of miracles,
Dazzlingly white flowers
Even if it's really a night's dream
A superdog in a dream that you can't help but love
White frost-like mongrel
It's a dream that says I miss you

한라 들꽃

곶자왈에도
움이 튼다

까마중 진득찰 도깨비바늘 엉겅퀴
산부추꽃 투구꽃 물매화 주홍서나물
한련초 여우구슬 달맞이 야고

이런 들꽃이
바위 *숨골에서 물이 흐르면
즐거이 피어오른다

*곶자왈: 제주 3,400m 지대
*까마중 이외; 제주 들꽃 이름
*숨골: 물이 나오는 곳

Halla wildflower 한라 들꽃

Gojjawal
I cringe

Crow's Needle Thistle
Mountain leek flower helmet flower water plum vermilion sprout
Nasturtium grass fox bead moon yago

Such a wild flower
When water flows from the rock *breath bone
It blooms joyfully

*Gojjawal : Jeju 3,400m
*Other than the crow; Jeju wildflower name
*Hide: Where the water comes out

죽심(竹心)

사시사철 푸른 기상이 물결처럼 넘쳐나고
흔들림에도 유유히 마음은 지조를 잃지 않았네
지난 일을 돌이키면 백설(白雪)을 견뎠고
詩를 즐기는 객이 또한 돌아갈 뜻을 잊었다네

竹心 죽심
四時常綠氣洋洋 사시상록기양양
搖興自舞不失强 요흥자무불실강
過路回想堪白雪 과로회상감백설
樂詩騷客依歸忘 락시소개의귀망

*한시: 칠언절구

a bambo of heart 죽심

The blue weather overflows like a wave in all seasons,
In spite of the shaking, my heart has not lost its grip.
Looking back on the past, I endured the snow white,
The one who enjoys the poem has also forgotten the intention of
returning.

竹心
四時常綠氣洋洋
搖興自舞不失强
過路回想堪白雪
樂詩騷客依歸忘

*Time: Seven Verses

가을 나그네

가을의 문턱에 서 있노라면
낙엽을 밟는 자가 있을 것이다
먼 산을 바라보듯이
묻지 마라, 어디로 가는 자인지
나이 어린 탓에 알 까닭은 없어도
아마 바람 불어 낙엽 따라 갈 것이다

계절 지나고 그 계절을 맞이하면
낙엽을 밟는 자가 또한 있을 것이다
그 자리에 낯선 자가 있다 해도
슬퍼 마라, 타인이기 때문이다
가을이 그대 이름을 부를 때까지
세월을 기다릴 줄 알아야 할 것이다

Autumn Traveler 가을 나그네

Standing on the threshold of autumn,
There will be those who tread on the fallen leaves
As if looking at a distant mountain
Don't ask, where are you going
Even if I don't know because I'm young
Perhaps the wind blows along the leaves

When the season passes and the season arrives,
There will also be those who tread on the fallen leaves
Even if there is a stranger in the place
Don't be sad, because you're someone else
Until autumn calls your name
You'll have to wait for the years

가을 편지 속을 터는 밤인데

가을밤은
깊어가고 물든 계절은 저절로 농익는데
가는 숨도 버거워 이 육신은 안팎으로
생명이 궁합니다

그렇습니다
더불어 익어가기엔 막다른 감성인 탓으로
나뭇잎에 빗물 떨어지는 소리
밤 내내 이어집니다
전등불 아래 책상 앞에 앉아 나는
모정의 향수에 먹빛 눈물을 흩날립니다

이 밤 다 새고 나면
모든 것 티끌처럼 사라질까 두려움에
살뜰한 추억 몇 가닥 감아
돌아올 시간의 호주머니에 훌쩍 접어두려는
이유입니다
빗소리는 점점 커지고
밀려드는 외로움 그런 그리움이
가을 단풍 속에 번지는 것과
바람에 이는 촛불을 가슴으로 감싸고 있는 일 같습니다

심장은 생잎처럼 타들어 가듯
연기로 솟습니다
감정은 조각난 돌멩이로 구르고
머리칼 한 움큼씩 가을 깊은 곳에 떨어지는 것
모든 속내를 툭툭 털어
고립된 깊은 심사를 손수 올립니다

이 비 강물 되고 바다로 다 와 가는
그 결만큼 이름들에 닿을 수 있다면
다하는 마음 깊이 새기어 놓겠습니다
이만, 청춘이 바래지는 비 오는 깊은 가을밤에 답장 없는 편
지를 남겨두렵니다

It's the night of the autumn letter,

가을 편지 속을 터는 밤인데

Autumn nights
The deepening and dying seasons ripen by themselves.
Even the thin breath is difficult, this body is in and out
Life is in short need

I do
It's too much of a dead end for me to ripen in addition.
The sound of rainwater falling on the leaves
It continues throughout the night
Sitting at my desk under the lamplight, I
Scatter dark tears in the perfume of motherhood

After the night is over,
Fear that everything will disappear like dust
Wrap up a few strands of tender memories
That's why you want to keep it in your pocket when you come
back

The sound of the rain is getting louder and louder,
The loneliness that creeps in, such a longing
Smearing in the autumn foliage
It's like holding a candle in the wind

My heart is burning like a raw leaf
It rises with smoke
Emotions roll into fragmented stones,
A handful of hair falling into the depths of autumn
Shake off all the insides
Raise the isolated deep examination by hand
This rain rivers and rivers come all the way to the sea

If you can reach the names as much as the grain
I will engrave it in my heart
I'm afraid to leave an unanswered letter on a rainy, deep
autumn night when my youth is fading

설야(雪夜)

백설 덮인 밤
찾아오는 이 없다

천 번이고 만 번을
한숨만 짓는다

긴 세월 가슴에 쌓이는
녹지 않은 모정

그 옛날
별이 잠시 떠오른다

동백꽃 향기
절로 풍겨 나온다

Snow Night 설야

Snow-white night
There is no coming

A thousand times and ten thousand times
I just sigh

Accumulated in the chest for a long time
Unmelted hair crystal

Those old days
The stars rise for a moment

Camellia fragrance
It exudes verses

장군(將軍)의 귀환(歸還)

—기억하라, 봉오동 전투

나라 잃고 낯선 이국(異國)에서
민족을 위하는 길을 찾아 일어섰다

남의 땅, 피눈물로 갈고 일구어
찢어지는 울분(鬱憤) 속에
약탈하는 적과 전투에 사활을 내걸고

'일당백(一當百)' 수천의 적군에 맞서
빗발치는 총탄(銃彈)의 사선 앞에
마지막 빛을 토해내는 별처럼
승리 아니고는 죽음밖에 없는 생과 사

범 같은 기질과
민족을 위한 동지들의 용맹과 큰 뜻을
드높은 하늘도 감동(感動)하였으니

'전장(戰場)의 적군은 고꾸라져 쌓이고 쌓여
산(山)과
붉은 강(江)을 이루었다' 라고

아, 봉오동 봉오동
그 날의 빛나는 승전보(勝戰報)
높은 하늘도 알고
깊은 땅도 알고 있다는
대승의 역사(歷史)다

*홍범도 장군이여
이 땅 위에 영원히 부르고 남을 이름이여

그 후,
이역만리(異域萬里)에 순국한 지 78년 만에
태극기에 포근히 감싸고
*대한(大韓)으로 귀환(歸還)
이것은 또한 승리가 살아 있는 전설이다

*대한: 대한민국의 준말
*여천 홍범도(1868.8~1943.10)장군 대한독립군총사령관
봉오동전투, 청산리대첩을 승리
*별세 78년 만에 고국으로 귀환 국립대전 현충원
제 3묘역에 안장함 (2021.8.15.)

The Return of the Generals 장군의 귀환

- Remember, Battle of Bong O-dong

Lost in a country and in a strange foreign land
He stood up to find a way for the nation

Someone else's land, plowed and cultivated with tears of blood
In the tearing resentment
Risking your life in battle with the plundering enemy

Against thousands of enemy soldiers
In front of the barrage of bullets
Like a star spewing out its last light
Life and death are the only things that can be done but victory

Bum-like temperament and
The valor and great will of the comrades for the nation
Even the lofty heavens were touched.

'The enemy on the battlefield is piled up and piled up,
Mountains and
formed a red river.'

Ah, Bong O-dong Bong O-dong
The day's shining triumphant telegram
I know the high skies too
That the deep earth also knows
It is the history of Mahayana

*General Hong Beom-do,
A name that shall be called and remain forever on this earth,

Subsequently,
After 78 years of martyrdom
Wrap it up in a Tai Chi Ki
*Return to Korea
This is also a legend in which victory is alive

*Daejeon: Short for South Korea
*General   Yeocheon   Hong   Beom-do   (1868.8~1943.10),
Commander-in-Chief of the Korean Independence Army
Battle   of   Bong   O-dong,   victory   over   Cheongsan-ri
counterintelligence
*Returned to his homeland after 78 years of death at the
National Daejeon Memorial Center
Interred at the Third Cemetery (2021.8.15.)

군화(軍靴)

포성(砲聲) 소리 산천을 흔드는 기세로
나는 명예로운 군인(軍人)이 되었다

훈련의 훈련은 천명의 기회
생명 같은 군번을 운명으로 받았다

푸른 제복의 뜨거운 가슴안에
조국의 이름으로 붉게 새겨 넣고
강산이 세 번 바뀌도록 나라를 위한
전투장에 피와 땀을 흘려가며 누비었다

지킬 산하를 심장에 품고
이어온 선열의 혼으로 막는 위국충정(爲國忠正)을
덧입어 유월 하늘,
오늘의 푸른 산하는 우리들의 얼굴이다

죽어 무덤까지 태극기로 보듬을 헌신(獻身)
호국으로 다시 이뤄낼 영혼까지
가만히 들어보라 귀 기울이면
천지를 밟는 천 년의 군화 소리

Military boots 군화

With the sound of gunfire shaking the mountain spring,
I became an honorable soldier

Training of training is a thousand opportunities
I was given a life-like military number as my fate

In the hot chest of the blue uniform
Engraved in red with the name of the motherland,
For the country so that the strong mountain changes three times
Blood and sweat spilled on the battlefield

With Jekyll in his heart
The spirit of glandular fever that has been prevented
Wear it on
June sky,
Today's green mountains are our faces
                                    Dedication to die and
take care of the grave with Tai Chi (獻身)
Even the soul that will rebuild the country

Listen
If you listen carefully
The sound of a thousand-year-old military boots stepping on
heaven and earth

풍유도 (백령도)

4부 인생만곡

The curvature of life

동백꽃 이름으로
살으셨습니다

당신은 그렇게 살으셨습니다

내가 이 땅에 발붙이길 아주 오래전에
돌계단을 오르는 한라산 아래 서서
세찬 눈보라에 나무람 없이
이날 도록 당신은 토박이로 지켜왔습니다

봄과 여름이 가을을 높이 사고
겨울이 와서 눈이 길 앞을 막아서는 세상에
가난과 추위와 외로움으로 죄어와
당신의 이치에 맞물려도 거역 없으셨습니다

빛이 길수록 동백잎 파릇해지고
향기 없이 꽃은 더 붉게 피어나
그 나무뿌리는 모질게 자릴 잡는 일
당신의 심지가 얼마나 깊어 가늠할지 모릅니다

쉴새 없이 바람의 언어는 온몸으로 꽂으며
붉은 꽃잎 지는 모습
처음처럼 끝까지 나약하지 않으셨습니다
그러므로 전율 돋는 이 말씀
아직도 또렷이 남아 격분이 일어 뜨겁습니다

'꺼져가는 화롯불 앞에 나를 앉혀놓고
누누이 옛일 전하는 당신의 눈물이 흐를 적에 삼촌들의
비참한 죽음과 숱한 이들의
제삿날로
역사의 날 선 총과 칼을 상상하였습니다
혼(魂) 씻기는 저 울린 가슴에 *추모(追慕)의 날은 이어
옵니다.'

폭풍설이 몰아오는 날은
살아온 날들보다 긴긴 천 년을 이어 뿌리 내린 삶
아, 어머니
층층이 쌓인 시간의 돌탑과
때마다 걸린 달과
땅 밑을 차 간절히 비는 그 말은
동백꽃 이름으로
살으셨습니다

*추모의 날 : 제주 4.3 희생자 (1948.4.3.~1954.9.21.)
*이 시는 제주 4.3 평화기념관 도서에 등록되어 보관중임

By the name of Camellia
you lived
동백꽃 이름으로 살으셨습니다.

That's how you lived

A long time ago I set foot on this earth.
Standing at the foot of Halla Mountain climbing the stone steps
Without blame in a fierce blizzard
To this day, you have been a native

Spring and summer make autumn look high
Winter has come, and the snow is blocking the way
Poverty and cold and loneliness
He did not disobey your reasoning

The longer the light, the bluer the camellia leaves become.
Without fragrance, the flowers bloom redder,
The roots of the tree are a rough harvest
You don't know how deep your wick will be

Without ceasing, the language of the wind is inserted into the whole body,
Red petals
He was not as weak to the end as he was at the beginning
Therefore, these words that make me shudder
It is still clearly visible, and the outrage is hot

'Sit me down before the burning fire,
When your tears flowed, the tragic deaths of your uncles and the many
Jesappalo
I imagined guns and knives on the day of history
The day of remembrance continues on the soul-washing chest.'

On a day when the storm is coming,
A life rooted for a thousand years, longer than the days lived
Ah, Mother
The layered stone towers of time and
The month that took each time and
The words that kick beneath the ground and pray eagerly,
By the name of Camellia
you lived

*Day of Remembrance: Jeju 4.3 Victims (1948.4.3.~1954.9.21.)
*This poem has been registered in the Jeju 4.3 Peace Memorial Museum Book and is being kept.

圃隱先生最後感
(포은선생 최후를 느끼며)

懷柔甘言三寸舌 회언감언삼촌설

丹心歌唱告終別 단심가창고종별

竹橋過際鐵槌衝 죽교과제철퇴충

忠節靈魂萬古烈 충절영혼만고열

회유와 감언을 세 치의 혀로 말을 해도
단심가를 부르며 종별을 고했네
선죽교를 지나는 즈음에 철퇴를 맞았으니
충절의 영혼이 만고에 뜨거워라

* 포은 정몽주 선생을 기리며
칠언절구 한시를 짓다

圃隱先生最後感
(Feeling the end of Mr. Po Eun)

懷柔甘言三寸舌

丹心歌唱告終別

竹橋過際鐵槌衝

忠節靈魂萬古烈

Even if you speak appeasement and exclamation with three tongues,
I sang a song and said goodbye.
As we passed the Seonjuk Bridge, we were struck with a mace.
Let the soul of integrity be hot in the midst of it.

* In memory of Mr. Chung Mong-ju
Seven Verses Han Poem

미궁(迷宮)

길은 없다
스스로 저울질할 수 없는 선택
한 길로 옆눈질 기웃댈 수 없이 가는 길
이뿐이다

숲이 우거져 나지 않은 길
돌짝과 엉긴 나무들과
움푹 팬 길가 물웅덩이 건너가는
거친 여정(旅程)이니라

다시 돌아갈 수 없는 별리(別離)에
가시밭길 밟은 발 뭉개지는 일처럼
옷소매에 눈물 훔치며 빛없는 침실에 갇힌
깊은 사정은
뼈아픈 슬픔
연주(演奏)뿐이다

오백 년 동백나무에 굳은 이 손이 닿기로
상처와 두려움이 주는 공허
찬바람이 스치는 동백잎 소스란 소리는
가야금(伽倻琴) 가락이 울린다

끝없는 손금의 길에 밤이 오고
그 밤이라야 별이 하나둘 떠오르는데
빈 악보(樂譜)를 보는 일은 미궁(迷宮)이다
남겨진 그 자리다

*황병기 가야금 미궁을 듣고서

Labyrinth (迷宮)

There is no way
A choice you can't weigh on your own
A road that you can't snoop on one side of the road
That's it

Unwooded roads
Stones and tangled trees,
Crossing a pothole of water on the side of the road
It's a rough journey.

In a place where there is no going back
Like the crushing of a foot on a thorny road
Stealing tears from the sleeves of his clothes, trapped in a
lightless bedroom
Deep ejaculation
Heartbreaking grief
It's just a performance

With this hand that has been hardened on the camellia tree for five hundred years,
The emptiness of hurt and fear
The sound of camellia leaf sauce in the cold breeze
The rhythm of the gayageum rings

Night is coming on the road of endless palmistry,
Only at night did the stars rise one by one.
Looking at a blank sheet music is a labyrinth
It's the spot that's left behind

*Listening to the Labyrinth of the 'Hwhang bueng ki'

녹슨 눈물

딱 정한 날 없이 가는
정(情) 닳은 문(門)이 있다

낯선 도시가 복잡하여도
한달음에 달려가고나

널친 마음에
녹슨 눈물
어머니 어머니는 조금이라도
편할까

Rusty tears 녹슨 눈물

Going without a fixed day
There is a well-worn gate

Even if an unfamiliar city is complicated
I'm running in a month.

Hearts and minds
Rusty tears
Mother, mother, even a little
Is it convenient?

어머니

어머니
나는 부릅니다

어머니 어머니
또 나는 부릅니다

어머니 어머니 어머니
자꾸만 나는 부릅니다

어머니의 이름을
잊지 않도록 나는 부릅니다

mother 어머니

mother
I call

Mother Mother
Again I call

Mother Mother Mother
I keep calling

Mother's name
So as not to forget, I call

YK에게 (그리운 벗에게)

하늘은 황사에 누렇다
이월의 끄트머리에 서성이며
꽃샘이 행패 부리듯이 봄을 시기한다

요즘에는
펜이 손에 무디어지고
책에서 눈을 뗀 지 안개 속이다

사실 하루가 금방 지난다
입 밖에 나오는 말보다
낯선 바람처럼 속도가 빠른 것 같다

몇 해 전부터 유행되는 팬더믹은 진정되지 않고
쌓여가는 걱정의 고지서에
삶은 피곤의 눈이 충혈된다

지금 나는
예전에 자네가 몹시도 생각나듯이
"고향은 잘 있겠지?"
징검다리로 흐르는 중랑천 개울물에
지나간 시간 돌려 등을 굽힌다

Dear YK (To a dear friend)

The sky is yellow with yellow dust
Pacing at the end of the carryover,
They envy spring like a spring of flowers

Nowadays,
The pen is dull in the hand,
It's been a long time since I took my eyes off the book and I'm
in the fog

In fact, the day goes by quickly
Than the words that come out of your mouth
It seems to speed up like a strange wind

The pandemic, which has been prevalent for several years, has
not subsided.
On the bill of worrying that is piling up
Tired eyes of life are bloodshot

Now I have
As I remember you terribly in the past,
"How's your hometown?"
In the stream of Zhonglang Stream flowing through the Jinggum
Bridge
Turn back the time that has passed and bend your back

홍우렁이

당신이 지나간 자리 너무 아름답습니다

폭설이 내린 날 방향 잃은 발자국
구멍 난 가슴에서 숭숭 기운이 빠져나갈 때

나 홀로 누운 곳에
서서히 온기가 스며들어와
노곤함을 재웁니다

또 행한 일 마음 아낌없이
밤새 눈길 터놓은 당신의 큰 업적(業績)을
나이 늦도록 알지 못하였습니다

Red worm 홍우렁이

The spot you passed is so beautiful

Disoriented footsteps on a day of heavy snowfall
When the aura of sublimeness escapes from the punctured chest

Where I lay alone
Warmth slowly seeps in,
Puts the sore to sleep

And what you have done, generously
Your great achievement that opened your eyes all night
I didn't know until late

먼 길

비가 철없이 와
창문을 덧댄 것
닫고 열기에
문틀 간이 닳아버렸습니다

먼 길
그대 오신다는데
자꾸 눈질 주며
청승맞게 빗방울만 헤고 있습니다

A long way 먼 길

The rain came without a beat
Putting up the windows
Close and open
The door frame is worn out

A long way
You're coming.
Keep giving me a glance
I'm counting the raindrops

별

나는 너에게
무엇이 될까

어둠을 밝히는
별빛이 되어야 할 것이고

너의 눈에
환한 미소로 비칠 때

바로, 너의 꿈이 되는
나는 별이 될 것이다

star 별

I tell you
What will it be?

Lighting up the darkness
It would have to be starlight,

In your eyes
When you shine with a bright smile

It's your dream
I will be a star

인생만곡(人生晚曲)

보라!
아름다운 정원에 고운 모습이여
그대는 한 줄기 빛을 받고
한 방울에 이슬을 마시며 사는
아름다운 생명이어라

꿀벌이 그대의 향긋한 향기를 맡고
찾아와서는
달콤한 꿀을 받고 쉬다가
날아가고 다시오는
그대 그대는 아름다운 꽃이어라

한창 그대는 아름다움을 만끽하는데
어디선가 찬바람이 일고
그대의 시련은 그 고통은
슬픔이여 애환이여

다가온 겨울에 몸서리치며
피려고 하려는
그대의 가냘픈 몸짓은 참으로
애처롭구나

오, 가엾은 영혼이여
찬란히 빛나던 생명이여
아름다운 그 날에 그대 모습은
오오, 푸르름이여
나 이제
그대를 위해 인생만곡(人生晚曲)을
부르리라

The curvature of life 인생만곡

Look!
A beautiful garden with a beautiful appearance
Thou shalt receive a ray of light,
Living with dew in a drop
It's a beautiful life

The bees smell your fragrant fragrance,
When I came to visit
Receiving sweet honey and resting,
Fly away and come back
Thou art a beautiful flower.

You are in the midst of beauty.
A cold breeze blows from somewhere,
Your trials are the pains of your trials.
Sorrow, sorrow,

Shuddering at the coming winter,
What you want to avoid
Your slender gestures are indeed
It's pathetic

Oh, poor soul
Life that shone brightly,
On that beautiful day, you will see
Oh, green,
I now
I will sing for you the curve of life.

꽃비에 바다가 그립다

시린 세월을 갉은 옹이에
싹이 튀어오는 날이면
그리움이 스미는 꽃비의 길을 따라
물길을 내어가고 있다

생각의 거리를 지나온 온갖 기억에
흩어진 추억들의 몸살을 앓듯
골짜기에 모여 얽힌 생각을 풀어
출렁이는 그리움의 바다로 가리라

아버지의 숨소리를 들으며
바위에 기대어 하늘을 들쳐 업고
별자리 헤이면 삶의 흔적을 밟아
어머니 얼굴을 가슴에 묻는다

노을에 잠긴 바다를 별 밭에 걸어
하얀 포말로 모래밭에 쏟아놓은
그리움의 사색에 바다가 그립다

I miss the sea in the rain of flowers
꽃비에 바다가 그립다

In the knots that gnawed through the years
On the day when the buds pop up,
Along the path of the rain of flowers where nostalgia is soaked
It's taking the water

To all kinds of memories that have passed through the distance
of thought
Like a whirlwind of scattered memories
Gather in the valley and unravel the tangled thoughts
Go to the sea of longing

Listening to my father's breath
Leaning against a rock and holding up the sky,
If you are a horoscope, step on the trail of life
I bury my mother's face in my chest

Walk the sunset-soaked sea in a field of stars
Spilled in the sand with white foam
I miss the sea in the contemplation of longing

모진 날이 지나고

선술집에 들러 술병이 쓰러질 때마다
가난한 마음을 털어놓는다

빈 의자에는
작고 큰 돌담이 쌓인 동백나무 한 그루가 선 옛날 집이
뭉텅 그려진다

설은 고독이 밀감같이 노랗게 익을 때쯤
뜨거운 감정이 끓어 오르는 것

처진 안경을 올리고
쓰러진 술병에 별을 담으며
웃는 날이 곧 오리란 걸 들려주고 싶다

모진 날이 지나고
꽃 피는 봄을 기다리며

After a terrible day
모진 날이 지나고

Every time I stop at a tavern and my bottle of liquor falls
Confess your poor heart

On an empty chair there is a
An old house with a single camellia tree with a small and large
stone wall is depicted

When the solitude ripens yellow like wheat
Boiling hot emotions

Raise your drooping glasses,
Putting a star in a fallen liquor bottle
I want to tell you that the day of smiling is coming soon

After a terrible day,
Waiting for the flowering of spring

양산 속의 여인

어느 여름 햇살 내리쬐는
성산포 해변이 눈부시다

연분홍 보랏빛 양산 속에
꽃같이 미소를 던지는 여인

하얀 파도 넘실대고
마냥 고운 발로 사뿐하다

어린 청춘이 멀어진 후에도
나는 가슴에 출렁인다

The Woman in the Parasol 양산속의 여인

One summer sunshine
Seongsanpo Beach is dazzling

In the pale pink purple parasol
A woman who smiles like a flower

Overflowing white waves
It's just like a fair foot

Even after the young youth is far away
I shudder in my chest

낮 달맞이꽃

짓무른 상처의
어둠 속
홀로
마음을 소독하던 밤

그 밤을
해장하듯이
쓰린 속 깊이
또 달래며 지새웠다

손톱 같은
빛,

그 빛을
이슬로 당겨와
낮 달맞이꽃
곱게 곱게 피었다

Daytime evening primrose 낮달맞이꽃

of crushed wounds
Dark
alone
A night to disinfect the mind

That night
As if dismantling
Bitter Depths
I was soothed again

Like a fingernail
light

The light
Pull it with dew
Daytime evening primrose
Finely bloomed

흔적(痕迹)

눈물이 모래 위를 자근자근 밟는다

그 사연의 흔적들이
그림자같이 고스란히 따라온다

간이 생기를 잃고 시커멓게 마른다

멀어진 벼리에 찍힌 감성이
수시로 들먹일 때마다
심장이 펄펄 끓어 올라와
바로 눈물로 때워 식히는 외로움이다

먼바다가 돌아와
눈물 자국을 긁어낸다

Traces 혼적

Tears creep on the sand

The traces of the story
It follows like a shadow

The liver loses its vitality and dries up

The sensibility stamped on the distant thunderbolt
Whenever I get caught up in it from time to time
My heart was pounding,
It's the loneliness that cools down with tears

The distant sea is back
Scrape away tear stains

5부 정낭의 빗장을 풀며
Unwinding the bars of the seminal vesicles

어부의 아들

내 어릴 적에 친구의
아버지는 고기잡이를 했답니다

오직 그의 아버지는 자식을 위해서라면
새벽부터 늦은 밤까지
거센 바다와 맞부딪쳤습니다

고기를 팔고, 그의 아버지는 그 돈으로
각가지 일용품 등을 사 오셨답니다

그의 누이는 오색종이로 배를 접고
그는 공책에 무어라 낙서를 했답니다

그의 누이와 함께 너무 행복에 겨워서
하늘에 계신 어머니의 얼굴조차 잊었답니다

몇 해 전에 그의 누이는 시집을 간 후
그는 조그만 도시에서 학교를 다녔답니다

차츰 그는 도시 생활에 익숙해져서
바다로 갈 생각을
미처 못했답니다

그는 방탕한 무리들과 속한 까닭에
그의 아버지의 옛 모습에
도무지 고개를 들고 다니지 못했답니다

그의 아버지 그의 어머니 그리고 그의 누이는
이젠 그의 삶에 관심을 가질 수 없답니다

예전에 그는 바다를 사랑하였으나
꿈속에서만 바라볼 뿐이랍니다

The fisherman's son 어부의 아들

of a friend from my childhood
His father was a fisherman

Only for his father's sake
From dawn until late at night
We ran into a raging sea

Selling meat, his father used the money
They bought all kinds of daily necessities

His sister folded her belly in colored paper,
He scribbled something in a notebook

With his sister, he was so happy,
He had forgotten the face of his mother in heaven

A few years ago, his sister passed away from her in-laws.
He went to school in a small town

Gradually, he became accustomed to city life.
The idea of going to the sea
He didn't

Because he belongs to the dissolute multitude,
In the old form of his father
He couldn't keep his head up

His father, his mother, and his sister can't take an interest in his
life anymore

Formerly he loved the sea,
He only sees in his dreams

가파도에서 본 풍경

바람의 강(江)

아주 먼 대대손손 내려주신 조상이
흐르는 강을 보라 한다

바람 *높은 산 그 아래 천지의 젖줄기
산과 사람을 휘돌아
이 나라 한라까지 푸른 빛 물살 출렁인다

아버지의 아버지
역사는 넘쳐 강을 이룬 것처럼
*다섯 강의 이름을 따라서
그 뒤를 *서른 소강은 한 핏줄로 모아 나선다

갈대의 속머리 허옇게 날리고
겨울새 날아오르면 봄꽃이 피는 날에
반만년의 시대를 이끌어
바람 흐르는 그 강으로 가자

'어디서 흘러
어디로 흘러가는 것인지'
강물의 숨통을 박동(搏動)하러 우리 가자

'강은 흘러야 산다'
한때 거칠고 험한 땅에서 정을 돋워
선량한 기운 산을 돌아 어디에서나 반긴다

더 낮아 겸허해지는
반만년 두터운 이야기 산천에 누이고
아버지의 가슴으로 오직 흘러보자

*높은 산 : 백두산
*다섯 강 : 압록강 두만강 대동강 한강 낙동강

*서른 소강 : 임진강 한탄강 북한강 남한강 소양강
홍천강 섬강 평창강 동강 주천강 금호강 형산강 밀양강 황강 태화
강 남강 금강 천내강 만경강 동진강 섬진강 영산강 보성강 황룡강
탐진강 예성강 청천강 허천강
부전강 장진강

River of the Winds 바람의 강

An ancestor who has passed down from generation to generation
Behold the flowing river

Wind *High mountains beneath them, streams of milk from
heaven and earth
Stirring mountains and people
The blue water rushes all the way to Halla, the country

Father's Father
History overflows like a river
*Following the names of the five rivers
This is followed by a lull in the *thirty lull

The hollow of the reeds blows away,
If it flies in winter, on the day of the spring blossoms
Leading the era of half a millennium
Let's go to that windy river

'Where does it flow
Where is it going?'
Let us go to beat the breath of the river

'A river must flow to live'
Once in a rough and rough land,
Round the mountains with a good aura, welcome everywhere

Lower and humbler
Half a millennium of thick stories lying in the mountain stream
Let it flow only to the Father's heart

*High mountain: Mt. Baekdu
*Five rivers: Yalu River, Duman River, Daedong River, Han River, Nakdong River

*Thirty lulls: Imjin River, Hantan River, North Korean River, South Han River, Soyang River
Hongcheon River Seomgang Pyeongchang River Donggang Jucheon River Kumho River Hyungsan River Milyang River Huanggang Taehwa River Nangang Geumgang Cheonnae River Mangyeong River Dongjin River Seomjin River Yeongsan River Boseong River Huanglong River Tamjin River Yesheng River Cheongcheon River Hecheon River
Buzhen Jiangjin River

눈물

늘 당신의 보답을 일구지 못해
손은 어디에 둘지 부끄럽습니다

당신의 호의를 높이 살 때마다
철 지난 감성이 무너져 내립니다

차가운 날일수록
불같이 기둥을 세웁니다

당신에게 선보일 수 있는 것
그것은 흐르는 마음입니다

tear 눈물

I can't always get you back
I'm embarrassed to put my hands

Every time I buy your favor highly
The sensibility of the past is crumbling

The colder the day, the more
Erect pillars like fire

What can be presented to you
It's a flowing mind

물 허벅질 하는 아이

물항아리의 물은 제 목숨줄과 같은 것
그 길로 오며 가며
아이는 가난한 살림 물 한 동 보태고
동전닢 한 개보다 적은 밥술을 떴다

돌작만 한 어깨에 물허벅은 파도보다 높아
발에 채여 물 한 겹 출렁이면
돌작만 한 심장도 같이 흔들리는데
그런 아이 진흙 같은 머리를
함박꽃 같이 웃으며 쓰다듬던 노모의 정

그 웃는 얼굴이 담긴 용천 물을
하늘과 구름과 해와 나뭇잎으로 길어
아이는 행복한 고생이 물결친다

물허벅 둘린 띠를 잡고 구슬치기 공놀이
장난질에 노는 아이들의 웃음소리 감자하여
물항아리에 가득 물이 차오르면
어머니의 웃음이 그 웃음에 섞이어
물항아리에 동전 소리 아이의 꿈이 출렁이었다

A child with water thighs 물허벅질 하는 아이

The water in the jar is like my lifeline
Coming and going in that way,
The child is a poor household and a bucket of water
I ate less than one coin

On the shoulders the size of stones, the thighs of the water are
higher than the waves
If you get stuck in your feet and run a layer of water
The heart that is the size of a stone shakes with it.
Such a child's muddy head
The old mother's affection that smiled and stroked her like a
flower

The spring water with that smiling face
Long with the sky and the clouds and the sun and the leaves
The child is in a wave of happy troubles

Holding a sash around the water thighs and playing ball
The laughter of children playing
in mischief potatoes
When the water jar fills up with water
My mother's laughter mingled with that laughter
The sound of coins in the jar of water, the child's dreams were
rushing

- 196 -

정낭의 빗장을 풀며

유년의 기억 너머
수평선을 당겨, 길을 여는 파도 소리
발끝의 호기심 따라 부딪히는
한림항 올레길 물비늘을 밟고 간다

에메랄드빛 푸른 정적 동심을 깨트리며
갈매기 울음으로 돌아가는 저물녘
어머니 밥 짓는 연기가 허기로 잦아들면
별들이 먼저 와서 *정낭의 빗장을 비춘다

드센 바람에도 웃음마저 곱게 담아
위안 삼던 아린 기억
어머니의 그리운 낮달로 걸어두고
외로운 물소리 헤이며
생생하게 흔들리는 그 바다를 건넌다

어머니의 흰 머리 풀어놓은 거친 세월을 감아올려
기댈 곳 없어도 아낀 정 무릎에 꺼내놓고
돌아와 천천히 걸어보는 올레길 집 앞

가로지른 세 개의 추억이 해풍만 가득하고
바람에 몸을 맡긴 너른 품새
달빛도 정낭을 품고 빗장을 풀고 있다

*정낭 : 제주도 옛집 출입문에 세 개의 나무통을 정주석에 끼거나
내려서 사람이 있는지 없는지를

Unwinding the bars of the seminal vesicles
정낭의 빗장을 풀며

Beyond Childhood Memories
Pulling the horizon, the sound of the waves opening the way
Bumping along the curiosity of the toes
Hallym Port Ole Gil steps on the water scales

Breaking the emerald blue static concentric
The twilight returns to the cry of the seagulls
When the smoke of cooking mother's rice fades away with
hunger
The stars come first and illuminate the bars of the seminal
vesicles

Even with a strong wind, even a smile is finely
Fond memories of Arryn
Hang it with my mother's nostalgic day moon
The sound of lonely water
Cross that vividly swaying sea

Mother's white hair rolled up the rough years
Even if you don't have a place to lean on, put it on your lap
Come back and walk slowly in front of the house

The three memories that crossed are full of sea breezes,
A generous bosom in the wind
The moonlight is also unravelling the bars with seminal vesicles

*Jeongsang: At the entrance door of the old house on Jeju
Island, three wooden barrels are inserted or lowered to check
whether there are people or not.

몽정(夢精)

바닷물이 가슴까지 차오르는
산꼭대기에 내리는 소나기 같은
그리움 때문일까

그 날밤 꿈자리에
아이는
못내 감정을 쏟아낸다

이부자리를 감싼
낯가림은
아야 밤이 길기만 하구나

Mongzheng (夢精)

The sea water rises to the chest
Like a shower on the top of a mountain
Is it because of nostalgia?

In a dream that night
The child is
I can't let my emotions out

Wrapping the futon
Strangeness is
Ouch, it's been a long night

만월 (FULL MOON)

세월에 論하여

가지 마라 가지 마라한들
네가 안가겠는가
석별(惜別)은 만남 뒤에
잠시 뜨는 별처럼
반짝이는 물빛같이 아리고

가지 마라 가지 마라한들
나만 두고 가겠는가
정(情) 들어도 스치는 바람과 같이
잠시 뜨는 달처럼 홀로 스러지는데

한 세상 아픔도 품어 살아갈 제
여보게, 세월(歲月)
고약하다 말고 붙잡을 수 없을 바에야
한판 신명 나게 살아봄도 낫지 않은가

About the years 세월에 논하여

Don't go, don't go, don't go
Won't you go?
After the meeting
Like a star that rises for a moment
Like the sparkling waters

Don't go, don't go, don't go
Will you leave me alone?
Like the wind that blows through the heart
Like the moon rising for a moment, it fades away alone

I'm going to live with the pain of the world
Honey, in the years
It's nasty, but I can't hold on to it
Isn't it better to live a bout of excitement?

신세 (身世)

먼 고향 바다 너머로
안부를 타진합니다

돌담 올레길 따라
아직 눈 안에 남아 있는지요

철쭉꽃 피는
한라산은 별고 없으신지요

한림항 고깃배는 새벽잠을 비비며
닻을 올려 바닷길을 열었는지요

술이 빈 잔을 채우고
탁자에 바다詩가 흐르지요

wretched life (身世)

Far away home, beyond the sea
Best regards

Along the stone wall trail
Is it still in the snow?

Azalea blooming
Hallasan is nothing special

Hallym Port Ferry rubbing the dawn sleep
Did they raise the anchor and open the way to the sea

Liquor fills the empty glass,
Sea poetry flows on the table

밤길에서

지친 바람이 허기진 잠에 곤히 들고
중랑역로 골목길 가로등이
담벼락 구석에 지새우는 희미한 밤이다

정원에 장미 나무는
덜 여문 망울이 꽃 피울 시간을 달래가며
검은 그림자는 잠옷 바지에 밤을 쫓아
비틀거린다

어느 곳에서
죽음이 검은 그림자 뒤를 쫓아와
폐부를 시리게 찌른다
생각의
잔여물이 길바닥에 홍건히 쏟아지고
또 생각이 죽었다
중랑천 건너 둑길은 너무 외롭다
이 밤에 진리를 찾아내고자
별은 스스로 빛을 내어 어둠을 몰아내고 있다

돌아가는 올레길이 아주 멀리 있다해도
그 길은 낯설지 않다 기억이 선명한 까닭이다
잠시 밤길에서
모든 것을 마중한다

On the road at night 밤길에서

The weary wind sleeps hungry,
Zhonglang Station Road alleyway street lights
It's a dim night in the corner of the wall

A rose tree in the garden
Soothing the time for the less female mantle to blossom,
Black shadows chase the night in pajama pants
Stumble

Where's the
Death chases after the black shadow,
Prick the lungs
Thoughts
The remnants are pouring down on the pavement,
Again, the thought died

The causeway across the Zhonglang River is too lonely
To find the truth in this night
The stars are dispeling the darkness by giving out their own
light

Even if the road back is very far away
The path is not unfamiliar, because the memory is clear

On the road at night for a while
Welcome to everything

밤비

밤부터 젖는다
이른 아침까지
젖는다

나무는
나무뿌리까지 젖는다

한 생의
발 닿은 곳
그립도록 젖는다

밤부터 젖는다
이른 아침까지
젖는다

night rain 밤비

It gets wet from the night
Until early morning
Get wet

The tree is
It gets wet to the roots of the tree

In a lifetime
Where to get your feet
I get wet so that I miss it

It gets wet from the night
Until early morning
Get wet

바닷길

바닷길
끊어질 듯 이어진다

한 발짝 내딛듯이 나의 마음속으로
걸어본다

내 눈을 뜨면 가고 싶은 길이고
내 눈을 감으면 보고 싶은 길이다

먼 고향으로 가는 길은
나의 마음이 헤지게 닳는다

Seaway 바닷길

Seaway
It goes on and on

As if taking a step, into my heart
Walk

When I open my eyes, it's the path I want to take.
If I close my eyes, it's the path I want to see

The road to a distant homeland
My heart wears out

젖가슴

솜털 같은 함박눈이 가슴을 덮고
시린 달 품어 꿈을 키운 유년이었습니다

동백꽃 돌담 집 여닫이문 옆에서
달빛에 비치던 당신의 얼굴
옷고름 풀고 내어 물리는 젖가슴
봄날 햇살처럼 따듯함이 스미어들었습니다

외로운 길에 눈물은 소나기같이 쏟아져
바다에 일렁이는 저 기억 끝에서
당신 앞에 엎드려 식어버린 심장 소리
희미하게 들려오는 것 같았습니다
'애야! 너 왔으니 나 이제 편안히 쉬련다'

그 고된 삶을 내려놓으시고
당신께서는 빛나는 별이 되었습니다

나뭇잎 갉아 먹은 세월에도
시절의 꿈을 잃지 않고
당신의 그 품속을 동경(憧憬)하는 일입니다

bosom 젖가슴

fluffy big snowflakes cover in my heart
It was a childhood that embraced the moon and nurtured dreams

Camellia stone wall next to the swing door of the house
Your face in the moonlight
Loosening pus and sucking bosom
The warmth crept in like the sunshine on a spring day

On the lonely road, tears pour down like showers
At the end of that memory that shimmers in the sea
The sound of a heart that has gone cold as it falls before you
It seemed to be faintly audible
'My dear! Now that you are here, I will rest in peace.'

Let go of that hard life,
You have become a shining star

Even after years of gnawing leaves
Without losing the dreams of the days
It is to yearn for your bosom

할머니의 버스

울퉁불퉁한 산간 길을 한 생이 그러했듯
비릿한 바다 내음 가르는 버스 창밖엔
수평선 너머 갈매기 자맥질이 버거워 보였다

헐떡이는 엔진 소리가 진회색 매연을
할머니 고무줄 바지를 펄럭이듯 가르며
흐릿한 추억 속으로 파문이 인다

철없던 까까머리 소년의 깔깔대는 동공 속에
단발머리 소녀의 뽀오얀 미소가
에메랄드빛 바닷물에 얼비치고 있었다

눈에 넣어도 아프지 않을 손주를 위해
좁쌀과 보리쌀 몇 되와
시계처럼 아침을 알리던 장닭 한 마리를
삼베 보자기에 싸서
한림 장에 내다 파시곤 하였다

오랜 세월 정 닳은 푸른 마을로
투덜대듯 달리던 버스가
별이 되신 할머니를 태우고
얼레빛 돋은 하늘을 바라보며 집을 향해
긴 경적을 울리며 가고 있는 듯 하다

Grandma's Bus 할머니의 버스

Like a lifetime on a bumpy mountain road
Outside the window of the bus with the smell of the fishy sea
Beyond the horizon, the seagulls
seemed overwhelmed

The sound of a panting engine makes dark gray fumes
Flapping through Grandma's elastic pants
Ripples through hazy memories

In the stubborn pupils of a black-haired boy
The immaculate smile of a short-haired girl
It was freezing in the emerald waters

For grandchildren who won't hurt to put it in their eyes
A few grains of rice and barley rice
A long-haired chicken that heralded the morning like a clockwork
Wrapped in burlap cloth
He used to sell them in the cold forest market

To a green town that has been worn out for a long time
The grumbling bus
Carrying the grandmother who became a star,
Looking up at the bright sky, towards the house
It seems to be going with a long horn

밤비 (여름날)

비가 내린다

창문 밖 어둠 속에서 그 소리는
한밤중 내 잠을 또다시 깨워
수면을 방해한다
내 기척에 로로가 놀라 일어나서는
불편 섞인 눈짓을 보내는 듯 했다
나는 비 내음을 맡고는 철없던 지난 기억의
서운한 물음에 내적인 미안함을 갖는다
밤새 내리는 비는 흘러가면
주워 담을 수 없듯
허무함에 남은 그 무엇보다 쓸쓸한 것
쓸쓸함에 젖는 마음은 추적거리는 시간에 속울음과 같
은 것이다
내 귀에 들리는 빗소리 자필로 새긴 날
깊은 밤에 서글피 울어 헤아리는
그 마음속으로 "고마워요" 아낌없이 주는 그대에게 들
려주고픈.

night rain

It's raining

In the darkness outside the window, the sound
In the middle of the night, wake me up again
Disrupts sleep
Lauro was surprised by my presence and stood up.
He seemed to give him an uncomfortable glance
I smell the rain and remember the past
I feel sorry for the sad question
When the rain that falls overnight passes away
I can't pick it up
The loneliest thing left of emptiness
A heart soaked in loneliness is like a whisper in the chasing time
The sound of the rain in my ears The day engraved with my own handwriting
Crying sadly in the deep night, counting
In my heart, I want to say "thank you" to you who give generously.

한림 바당

제주 서쪽 해안도로를 따라오면
비양도가 보이는 한림항에 속한 바당
해 오르는 속도를 늦게서야 감지한다

그곳에 화살촉 같은 검은 바위와
토박이는 사투리를 고집하며 살고 있다

중천에 떠오른 해가 한라산 아래
삶을 잇대는 우엉밭에
유채꽃 콩꽃 깨꽃 감자꽃 메밀꽃
순서대로 피어
어머니의 은발을 타고 땀방울이 수십 갈래로 넓은 앞바
다에 전설처럼 흐른다

종달새 하늘 위로 정겹게 날아오르면
외방 간 자식의 감감한 소식에 그 가슴 속에는 날마다
사연이 검정 보말처럼 모였다

석양은 익어 바다는 오지게 타오르다가
숯처럼 날이 까맣게 되면
어머니의 무릎 위에 별이 되는 곳

그 별을 바라보며 한림 바당은
별빛을 받으며 파도가 검은 바위를 철썩인다

*한림 바당 : 한림 바다

Hallim Badang

If you follow the coastal road west of Jeju, you can see the speed of the Badang Sea, which belongs to Hallym Port, where you can see Biyangyang
There, black rocks like arrowheads, and the natives live in a dialect The sun rises in the middle of the sky, and in the burdock field where life continues under Halla Mountain
Rape blossoms, bean blossoms, sesame flowers, potato blossoms, wheat blossoms bloom in order, and beads of sweat flow like dozens of branches on the mother's silver hair, and when the lark soars lovingly above the sky, the story gathers in her heart like a black pumal every day at the heartbreaking news of her child who has gone away

The setting sun is ripe and the sea is burning fiercely, and when the day is black like charcoal, it becomes a star on the mother's lap, looking at the star, Hallym Badang is bathed in the starlight, and the waves lap the black rocks

*Hallym Badang : Hallym Sea

PHOTO BY KIM JONGCHEOL

한림항 Halllim port

새벽이여

목메는
붉은 설움

저 十字星이
어둠 한 곳에
비추고,

먼 이를
나는 찾는다

아침 쫓는
새벽이여!

*十字星 : 남쪽 하늘 별. 고향. 상명里

daybreak (새벽이여)

Thirsty
Red tongue

That cross star
In the middle of the darkness
Illuminate,

Distant teeth
I look for

Chasing the Morning
Dawn!

*十字星: Southern sky star. Sangmyung 里

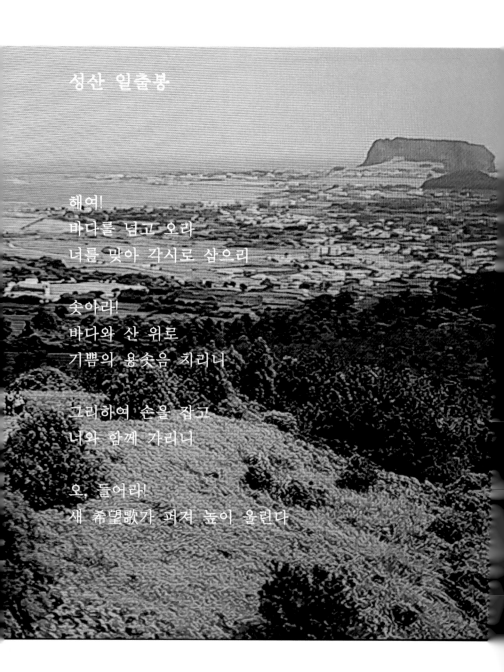

성산 일출봉

해여!
바다를 넘고 오라
너를 맞아 각시로 삼으리

솟아라!
바다와 산 위로
기쁨의 용솟음 치리니

그리하여 손을 잡고
너와 함께 가리니

오, 들어라!
새 希望歌가 퍼져 높이 울린다

Seongsan Ilchulbong 성산 일출봉

sun!
Come over the sea
I will receive thee and make thee my gaksi

Soar!
Over the sea and mountains
The Fountain of Joy

So, holding hands,
I will go with you.

Oh, listen!
A new chant spreads and rings high

호미 (Mother homi)

고부린 등 뒤로 뒷짐 지고
돌밭으로 나서는 어머니
햇볕 그을린 손에 흙 묻은 호미를
삼백예순다섯 날 중에 들지 않는 때가 없다

해가 떠오르고 해가 지도록 돌 찬 밭이랑에
검질을 매고 희망을 일구며
구부러진 호미는 고개를 숙일 줄 알면서도
절로 굴하지 않고 세상의 들판을 바라본다

비록 돌밭에 호미질하는 소리가
구성진 노랫가락이 아니라 할지라도
그 전설의 이야기가 새겨지듯
가슴에 메아리 된다

햇살이 무수히 쏟아지고
종달새 동백나무 우듬지 높이로 지저귀고
호미 앞에 땀눈물이 뚝뚝 떨어져 모이면
젖은 호미에 까맣게 흙이 묻어
흙 한 줌을 떼어낼 때마다
어머니의 등허리가 그 호미처럼 닳아간다

비가 오고 바람이 모질게 불어올 때
모든 것들이 쓰러져가는 일에
호미 날이 무뎌지도록 일으켜 마주하며
한숨을 낮추고
안중에 절망을 두려워 않는다

잿빛 하늘엔 먹구름이 다시 흐르는데
흐른 세월을 품은 어머니와
항상 흙 묻은 호미는 녹이 들지 않고
아, 돌밭 땅에 꽂혀 소임 다하는
그 순간마저도 한평생 말없이
아주 오랜 벗으로 남는다

Homie (Mother homi)호미

Carrying a burden on your back
A mother steps out into a stony field
Homie with dirt on sunburned hands
There is not one of the three hundred and sixty-five days that
is not included

In a stony field where the sun rises and the sun sets,
Tie up the sword and raise hope,
The crooked homie knows how to keep his head down, but
Undaunted, he looks at the fields of the world

Although the sound of homing on the stony ground
Even if it's not a composed song
As the story of the legend is engraved
It echoes in the chest

The sunshine is pouring in countless ways,
A lark chirps at the height of a camellia tree
When sweat and tears drip down in front of Homie
Wet homie with charred dirt
Every time you remove a handful of dirt
My mother's back looks like that homie

When it rains and the wind blows fiercely
On the fall of all things
Raise up and face the homie blade so that it may be dulled,
Lowering the sigh,
Don't be afraid of despair in your heart

The grey sky is full of dark clouds again.
With a mother who embraced the years gone by
Always a dirty homie does not rust,
Ah, stuck in the stony ground, doing all the work
Even at that moment, I was silent for the rest of my life.
Remain longtime friends

제주의 오름

수많은 오름 터기 위에
그들은 끊임없이 쉬지 않고 오르내린다

한 생이 나고 자라고
젖은 발자국이 마른 그 날까지

雪寒과 비바람을 몰아오는
모진 추위와 태풍에도
땡볕에 속이 시커멓게 타 들어가도
바위처럼 굳은 세월을 몸살 나게 견뎌왔다

한라산을 거저 오르지 않았다면,
제주 오름의 참모습이 솔직히 닿는다

*제주 오름은 368개

Oreum of Jeju 제주의 오름

On top of a multitude of Oreumteogi
They constantly go up and down without a break

A life is born and grows,
Until the day when the wet footprints dry

Storming and rainstorming
Even in extreme cold and typhoons
Even if your stomach burns in the sun
It has endured years as hard as a rock

If you hadn't climbed Halla Mountain freely
The true face of Jeju Oreum can
be honestly reached

*Jeju Oreum is 368

의군(義軍)의 총(銃)
― 안중근 장군을 위하여

탕,

탕,

탕....

의군(義軍)의 총(銃)이

원흉의 가슴에 심판(審判)하였다

새빨간 피 터진 폭도 *이등(伊藤)은

불지옥 앞에 고꾸라졌다

러시아 하얼빈역(驛)

1909년 10월 26일 10시

그날의 역사는 독립의 신호탄을 쐈다

대한 독립 만세

대한 독립 만세

대한 독립 만세

삼창은 단지의 맹서(盟誓)
'위국헌신군인본분(爲國獻身軍人本分)'

난국의 영웅은
민족(民族)을 위하여
정의(正義)가 살아 하늘이 통하였다

죽음 앞에서도 거치른 모습
억압과 핍박에서 자유의 평화를 위했다

그 이름 만대(萬代)에 알리라
'의군 안중근이여!'

* 의군(義軍) : 안중근 의병 참모중장

* 폭도 이등(伊藤): 이토 히로부미
  (안중근 장군에게 척결됨)

* 위국헌신군인본분: 나라가 위험에 처하면
군인의 본분을 다한다

The Gun of the Righteous Army

For General Ahn Jung-geun

soup
soup
Soup....

The guns of the righteous army
Judgment was placed on the chest of the original chest

Bright red bloody mob *Second class
I was bowed down in front of the fiery hell

Harbin railway station, Russia
October 26, 1909, 10 p.m.
The history of that day shot the signal for independence

Long live independence for Korea
Long live independence for Korea
Long live independence for Korea

The Three Spears are the oath of the complex
"Duty of a Dedicated Soldier to the Nation "

The hero of the impasse
For the sake of the nation
Justice prevailed, and the heavens prevailed

Tough in the Face of Death
For the peace of freedom from oppression and persecution

His name shall be known to all generations.
'Ahn Jung-geun! '

* Ui-gun (義軍): Lieutenant General Ahn Jung-geun Medical Staff
* Mob Second Class (伊藤): Ito Hirobumi
  (Redirected from General Ahn Jung-geun)
* Duty of a Dedicated Soldier: When the country is in danger
he do my duty as a soldier

This heart of mine that is held
붙들린 이 내 마음은

departed
Distant homeland

pass by Youth
Always in that memory

Sit quietly
Grab my Blunt breasts

Halla Mt.

The Way of Life 인생길

The Endless Road I walk

I'm on this road
Even if someone stops it
I'll go straight

Encountering along the way
A lot of things
Even in heavy snow and showers
Even under the scorching sun
Dressed in ragged clothes
I will walk

In your love Energizing
I have gray hair and it all falls out,
Even if the knee bone is worn out and the pain is numb
In your love
I will finish it at once.

I'm one 나 하나가

I'm one
Hardened by a ferry
Let me allow you to cross this deep river

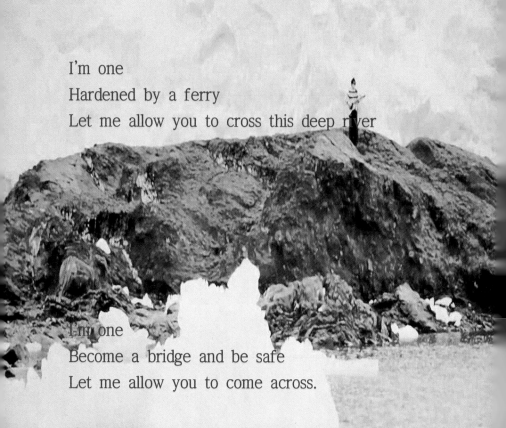

I'm one
Become a bridge and be safe
Let me allow you to come across.

If one of me wears a different body
With it
Because you are the way to come to me

In the Forest of Youth 청춘의 숲에서

When passing through the forest,
stop at the thick fragrance
Unknown nature is motley
You're close to me.

Everything is full of mystery
No more deep into the woods
I couldn't go.

Why can't I stay there?
Because I still have a lot of youth left in me
It was because

청춘에게

가격을 매겨 제 영혼을 팔려 한다면
청춘의 낭만이 아니지 않은가?
움츠리지 말고, 먼저 행동해라
네가 후회하지 않는 것
뜨거운 가슴을 던져
포기 없는 것
모진 세상의 바람 속에서
당당하게 말해라!
너의 길을 가는 것

To the youth

If you try to sell your soul at a price
Isn't that the romance of youth?
Don't flinch, act first
What you don't regret
Throw hot in your heart
No Giving Up
In the winds of the harsh world
Speak up!
Going your own way

[채당 연보]

1966년 7월 2일 제주도 출생. 본명 홍영길
1973년 금악초등학교 입학
1979년 한림 중학교 입학
1982년 한림 공업고등학교 입학
1986년 해병대 입대
1987년 해병대 부사관 교육 (정보 통신병과)
1996년 제주전문대학 受學
1998년 결혼 (강지윤)
2002년 경주 위덕대학 受學
2016년 해병대 제대 (예:원사)
         대통령 표창 수여
2016년 춘추 문예 시인 등단. 담쟁이 문학 이사
2018년 한국 낭송문예 협회 시낭송 지도자 수료
2021년 (천 년 같다는 말) 첫 시집 발표.
         (한라산 편지) 발표.
         (서울의 달) 발표.
2022년 (동백꽃 이름으로 살으셨습니다) 발표.
         (해운대 연가) 발표.
2023년 (흰 여우와 꽃과 시인) 발표.
         (클래식의 시작)
2024년 (한라아리랑) 한영 시선집 발표.
2024년 (한가락 가야금) 선생 한수진 침향무 受學

[Annals of Bonds]

Born July 2, 1966 in Jeju Island. Real Name: Hong Young-gil
1973 Entered Geumak Elementary School
Entered Hanlip Junior High School in 1979
1982 Entered Hallym Technical High School
Enlisted in the Marine Corps in 1986
Marine Corps Noncommissioned Officer Training in 1987
(Information and Communication Corps)
1996 Studied at Jeju College of Technology
2002 Gyeongju Wideok University Mathematics
Discharged from the Marine Corps in 2016 (e.g. yarn)
2016 Spring and Autumn Literary Poet Award. Director of Ivy
Literature, Awarded the Presidential Citation
2018 Korean Recitation Instructor
2020 Worked at the National Museum of the Japan Meteorological
Agency
In 2021, he released his first collection of poems (like a thousand
years).
　　　　(Hallasan Letter) announced.
　　　　(Seoul Month) announcement.
2022 (You lived under the name of Camellia Blossom) announced.
　　　　(Haeundae Annual Release) announced.
2023 (The White Fox and the Flower and the Poet) announced.
　　　　(The beginning of the classic) announcement.
2024 (Halla Arirang) announced.
2024 (Hangarak Gayageum) Teacher Han Sujin chimhyangmu 受學

Halla Arirang

Foot row|09 Jan 2024
Author| Chedang Hong Young-gil
Published by|Han Geon-hee
Photographer: Jiyoon Kang,dong whan Hong
painter: heami Hong, chedang
Published in|Bukk Co., Ltd.
Publisher registration|2014.07.15. (No. 2014-16)
Main office|서울특별시 Geumcheon-gu gasan digital 1ro 119
SK Twin Towers Building A Room 305
Telephone|1670-8316
Email|info@bookk.co.kr

ISBN | 979-11-410-6477-8
www.bookk.co.kr

한라아리랑 (Halla Arirang)

발   행 | 2024년 01월 09일
저   자 | 채당 홍영길
펴낸이 | 한건희
사 진 | 강지윤,홍동환
그 림 | 홍혜미,채당
펴낸곳 | 주식회사 부크크
출판사등록 | 2014.07.15.(제2014-16호)
주   소 | 서울특별시 금천구 가산디지털1로 119 SK트윈타워 A동 305호
전   화 | 1670-8316
이메일 | info@bookk.co.kr

ISBN | 979-11-410-6477-8
www.bookk.co.kr